I WAS JOKING, OF COURSE

PAUL JENNINGS

I Was Joking, Of Course

MAX REINHARDT
LONDON

❡ Acknowledgements

I am grateful to the Editor of *Punch* for permission to reprint *Love in the Design Centre, Nootalk, Giving up Sailing, England, What Do You Mean, a Rag Rf?, Scenario for Young Lovers, 1066 and All Saxon, All's Ill that Ends Ill, Riders to the Playboy, Suffolk, Wash Me in Steep-down Gulfs of Liquid Mr Sands!, The Downgrading of Gibraltar, The Unforgiving Second*; and to the Editor of the *Observer* for permission to reprint the remainder, which with the exception of *The Last Train to St Petersburg* and *Singing is so Good a Thing* appeared in the column *Oddly Enough* which I wrote until leaving that paper.

P.J.

This collection of pieces
© Paul Jennings 1968
SBN 370 00415 9
Printed and bound in Great Britain for
Max Reinhardt Ltd
9 Bow Street, London W C 2
by C. Tinling & Co., Ltd, Prescot
Set in Linotype Plantin
First published 1968

❡ Contents

CONTENTS

OVERTURE

❨ Wad Him a Lubly Barf

◆◆◆◆◆◆◆◆◆◆◆◆◆◆◆◆◆◆◆◆◆◆◆◆◆◆◆◆◆◆◆◆◆◆◆

IT *would* have to be my friend Harblow who noticed that my dog, Barker, had fleas. Deep down, he thinks we don't love Barker enough. He is not as bad as those bulky women, somehow recalling honest walking Welsh dressers, with agressively calm faces, a combination of JP and Earth Mother, who purse their lips when one speaks sharply to one's child in a crowd (how would *they* stop it trying to withdraw its hand and get lost? Sing to it? Recite from the *Bhagavad Gita*?): but undoubtedly he doesn't realize that with Barker you have to keep love under control.

Barker is a spaniel with a big silly heart and no mind, who howls whenever the telephone rings; he thinks it is something harsh and unloving from the outside world coming to break us all up. He is a kind of love-diabetic, everything turns to sugar unless we balance him with the insulin of gruffness. Drop gruffness for a moment and Barker puts his head on you, in the way Harpo Marx used to give unwary bystanders his leg to hold.

We have gruffly spent a great deal more on a kind of dogs' Harley Street treatment for Barker—operations on his ears, men in white coats, mysterious swab-cultures analyzed in Cambridge laboratories (and for all I know learned articles in the dogs' *Lancet*)—than we have on our children. No doubt it is a nice change for Harblow to have an adoring dog's head on his lap for a weekend.

7

His own dog, Jim, is hated and feared by his friends, it eats their gloves, growling to itself, and won't let them pass on the stairs. Once Harblow tripped up when he was taking it for a walk and it bit him on the ankle. There's nothing at all wrong with Jim, but it (Jim is *it*, not *he*) acts like someone, or rather something, with toothache; God knows what it would be like if it had been through Barker's troubles. We know Barker is a dog-saint—one of the more flamboyant, Counter-Reformation ones he would be, depicted in dramatic attitudes, ears flying, on baroque ceilings. But we can't tell him so unless we want his head on us.

Well, we gruffly saved his life, or at least these men in white coats did, but full cure was impossible and we had just come to accept the scratching. But Harblow, rubbing his head, said: 'Wad him a lubly Parper, den. Oosh, oosh. Aw, de him, wad him matter? Aw, Parper' (looking closely), 'him dot *fees*.'

And so he had. Only one thing to do; an insecticidal shampoo. And only one place to do it; in the bath. I always have a feeling that shampooing one's dog in one's bath, while the Chinese are making all those dams and steelworks, smacks of Western decadent affluence. But of course it would be even *more* decadent-affluent to buy a tin bath specially for this. (At least I wouldn't be like the woman I saw outside Harrods, with a dog wearing a tailored coat; every time it wagged its tail it came out of the special hole for it and she kept putting it back. I bet she had a special dog's bathroom, with dog's dressing-gowns and, if it was a bitch, black powder for its nose.)

8

'Tum on, Barper,' he said when we had draped the bathroom with old sheets and towels, 'gib him lubly barf. Esh *esh*. Wuzha den. Dere, him a goo boy. Tand up, like a goo boy.' For Barker knew what was coming. I've heard of water spaniels, but Barker is a land spaniel, he crouches and shivers in the bath before we've even started.

'Now, where de shishus an lubber glubs?' There were layers of stuff like felt, or the under-side of lino-leum, all over Barker, especially his ears (although both we and the men in white coats had done our best quite recently): I gave Harblow the scissors and rubber gloves, but he was no better than I was at gauging where this stuff ended and Barker began. There was a startled yelp and Barker skated round the bath, clanking on the enamel as with a hundred paws.

'Gib *me* the glubs,' I said. I got as much off as I could, producing the familiar tufted effect which is all one can hope for. On the bottle of shampoo it said *pour over dog in small quantities and work well into coat avoiding the eyes*, but of course it was impossible to avoid Barker's eyes, fixed on us with his *St Barker-Commends-His-Torturers (Mannerist-School)* look.

And then the telephone rang. Already depressed, Barker really made with the ululations: whatever it was, it was going to 'get us this time'. It put Harblow off such guard as he had, and when I went to answer the phone Barker saw his chance; he leapt out of the bath and followed me into the room. After previous baths the kitchen has always seemed too small and carpetless for what Barker wants to do. This was more like it. He

9

rushed round and round, pausing to shake himself or go along the carpet on three legs, one front knee and an ear, saying er ROOyer erROOyer, erROO. He shampooed the whole place. In a way I could quite see why Harblow, when he finally caught him and got a towel round him, far too late, said 'Ah, wuzha cleber Barper, wad him lubly barf.' He knew what would happen if he ever tried to get Jim near a lubly barf.

⁋ Erban Development

◆◆

IN MANY fantasies about computers taking over they simply appear as super human beings. One practically sees them walking about on little tin legs encased in boots which they have *chosen,* since value-judgment, imagination, creation, have been added to the other abilities in which they already so much exceed us—those of memorizing, classifying, problem-solving.

Only the other day I listened to an absolutely riveting BBC programme in which an I.B.M. 7090 at the Bell Telephone Laboratory, sounding exactly like a steam organ, played a Fantasia by Orlando Gibbons. Then it moved on to Pergolesi. When its attendant fed a bit of 'random' into it, during the few moments it took to detect the intrusion it played weird, inside-out Pergolesi. One imagined a part of it writing a 30,000-word life of Pergolesi, checking this with all known scores, flashing messages to another part UNPLAY CRESI PERGO-LESI REJECT RANDOM: then it got the Pergolesi right again.

At the end, accompanying itself on itself as a piano, it sang *Daisy, Daisy* in an endearingly moronic voice. It was impossible not to like it, one saw it back in some boring bank or steel mill making absent-minded mistakes about dividend ratios or furnace temperatures, boasting about Pergolesi to the other computers in the office, ringing up agents and trying to get an audition at the Met.

But, of course, this is not at all how computers will

take over. They won't bother with beating men at individual tasks like writing music (although I have often
wondered if they weren't having a go in some of those
Thursday Invitation Concerts). They will initiate vast,
complex social schemes of their own; and I am pretty
sure they have already embarked on one such—the re-
building, if that is the word, of London.

Almost without noticing it we have passed from the
old human days, when a new building was a definite
and isolated event, a rarity among the familiar network
of old grey stone mansions, leafy squares, lamp-posts,
alleys, wharves remembering Elizabethans and Romans.

Now, on any cross-London journey, one sees this old
life, forced to appear ever more eccentric and Dickensian (from bus or taxi windows I see defiant, pathetic
human signs: DAY AND NIGHT PLEATING
SERVICE: COMMERCIAL AND HERALDIC EN-
GRAVING in ghettoes of disappearing craftsmen), as
it is squeezed into isolated triangles between huge
blocks going up in mad profusion, the work of ERB
(Electronic Random Builder).

Human programmers, if there ever were any, have
long since disappeared. No one in an old building now
quite knows if or when it is to be demolished. People
walk along old brown corridors that end in blank sheets
of hardboard, from sashed windows they stare down at
bulldozers and up at huge cranes, uncertain whether
this is a new extension of their own firm or something
quite other. At the heart of this proliferation sits ERB
clicking and humming Pergolesi to itself, issuing
printed slips which bewildered medium-grade execu-

tives find themselves translating into signed orders directing a thousand insurance clerks here, a thousand typists there.

There are occasional errors; a nought is added by mistake to the height (in yards) of the new Post Office tower, tea 'boys' are grandly given £42 a week. But on the whole ERB takes good care to preserve the appearance of human control, to lull us until it is too late. Its word-association unit, for instance, has produced a whole list of names for building firms which are extraordinarily convincing, in a synthetic kind of way.

Thus, at about the fifteenth storey of new buildings in progress, we see large signs, often neon-lit at night, saying ACROW; obviously from the Greek *akros*, topmost (cf. *acropolis*). CUBITTS, with its biblical overtones, takes us right back to the Tower of Babel. More personal images are called up by ERB creations MINTER and TROLLOPE & COLLS.

These represent two balancing opposites. Trollopes and colls (or *cullies*) are from a bustling Shakespearean world of lusty building apprentices, mortar-scrapers dinging, bawdy songs ringing in the bright morning air, and their buxom wenches; minters, on the other hand, are grave, dignified Holbein figures weighing gold in little dark rooms.

ERB also sets itself to find a modern father-figure name suggesting at once craggy, honest reliability, social status, northern (indeed Scottish), solidity, and mountainous pure height. It came up with the masterly SIR ROBERT McALPINE.

But most significant of all are the names on a board

at a building site in Kingsway, and doubtless many other places: it says MACWEENEY & SMALLMAN, Demolition Contractors. Macweenies and smallmen are surely from basic northern mythology, part Teutonic and part Erse; little bearded creatures scampering about under the earth, hacking at iron pillars with dreadful little tinkling tools of magic power, skipping away with elvish glee as they bring yet another great building tumbling down in a crash of stone and dust; trolls carousing under our lighted halls, like the ones in 'Peer Gynt.' ERB had better watch out before *they* take over the programming.

ℂ Love in the Design Centre

◆◆◆◆◆◆◆◆◆◆◆◆◆◆◆◆◆◆◆◆◆◆◆◆◆◆◆◆◆◆◆◆◆◆◆◆◆

IT WAS raining hard when the two men came out from
Scott's after lunch. Jack Prode was thirty, rather bony,
with black crewcut hair crowning a face at once keen and
somehow nondescript. The high forehead, tight skin,
restless eyes and sharp jaw none the less left an impression simply of a big vague well-kept face, like a
cinema close-up of an unmemorable actor, or well-
defined rocks glimpsed and forgotten from a car window
abroad. He wore a good, fairly international-looking
raincoat. To see him at any airport in the Western world
it would have been difficult to guess whether he was
coming home or just leaving it. In fact he had grown
up in Wolverhampton.

In any pair or group there is always one who takes
the initiative even in a matter like obtaining a taxi. It
was Prode who led the way towards Piccadilly Circus so
that he could peer anxiously into more than one line
of traffic, scorning the umbrella which his companion
Andrew Ogilvie had opened over them.

Prode did this partly because to get wet in this day
and age seemed the kind of insult life ought no longer
to proffer one who had risen so far from an elementary
school education; partly because he had to be at a zinc-
yard in Plaistow by 2.45; and partly because he was
half afraid that after all his efforts Ogilvie, with no
exertion at all, would suddenly say *Taxi!* in his well-
bred, managerial voice, and one would slide up to the
kerb out of nowhere. Ogilvie was Phoenix Develop-

ment Ltd., and over the lunch the two had agreed on a contract whereby many muddy lorries and smart vans bearing the name PRODE would soon be carrying a wide range of building fixtures and equipment to certain huge new blocks of flats and offices.

'It's no good, Prode. The blighters sit drinking tea in those little green sheds they have on the pavement when it's raining. Relax. Let's pop into the Design Centre. I hear Milo Perkins has some wonderful new taps. Might be in your line.' He eyed Prode quizzically.

Blast him, thought Prode. Prufitt, his Plaistow manager, would be waiting for instructions on the new consignment of mandrils, turpins, bobbins, bushes, barrel unions, chromium and brass bibcocks and Supatap cocks. He resented the way Ogilvie and so many others dragged their art education into business. And these *designers*! Teapot yesterday, some fool chair today, telephone tomorrow; make a fancy shape, then some poor devil of a technician has to fit the works in. But he only said 'Good idea!' He could not bring himself to add 'Ogilvie.'

As Ogilvie was shaking his umbrella on the threshold of the Design Centre, Prode glanced inside and fell in love for the first time in his life. Standing by some black coffee cups was a very neat, smallish girl with enormous eyes, a soft fall of hair, and lips that seemed both neat and wild.

'Mitzi, my love!' cried Ogilvie. 'Divine to see you! This is me friend Jack Prode. Mitzi Slade-Bennett. One of the greats, Prode, one of the greats.'

Patronizing swine! He wants her to think I'm a peasant, thought Prode.

'Delighted, Miss Slade-Bennett,' he said in a deliberate voice. 'I've read a great deal about your grafting of English surface decoration on to Scandinavian clarity and the resultant fusion into a highly personal yet detached and cool style.'

A new look flickered in Mitzi's ambiguous eyes. There was something angry, something curious, something proud, something appealing, and something obscurely maternal in it. And something sexual. A look boding involvement. A look with *thou* in it.

'Are you a hard man, Mr Prode?' Her voice was slightly husky. Ogilvie was already less real than either of them, for stars had collided. From far away already his voice seemed to come. 'Well, my dear, what are you showing?'

'Nothing much.' Mitzi's eyes never left Prode's. 'A few flat pin switch socket outlets, and a rather amusing little fused spur unit in moulded plastic, for flush fitting.'

They paused in front of a chaste bed-sitting room apparently belonging to a geological student who drank, for there were tall glasses containing lumps of quartz and other rocks, several bottles of stout, maps on the walls, a chair with matching footstool, presumably for use when the fumes of stout overcame concentration. On the bedside table, integral with the bed, was the *Penguin Book of Sick Verse*. Little cards on the guard rail gave details of the design and provenance of these objects.

Mitzi said 'There's something pure about geology.'

Prode held her gaze levelly. 'I like a bedroom to look *lived* in,' he said. 'And what the hell do they mean, *vanitory unit*? It's just a wash-basin and some shelves.'

'Andrew seems to have gone. God, I could do with a coffee.'

'I am going to be the first man to ask for it at the Tea Centre. Come on.'

Not up the Haymarket and Jermyn Street did they go on that short first walk; but through forests, seas, dawns, twilights, magical morning fields haunted by strange birds, voices, bells.

Mitzi said 'I'd *rather* have tea. Then take me to your zinc-yard.'

'Can you fight?' Prode's voice held weariness. 'It will be necessary; I am going to love *you*, not what you do. My world holds Prufitt as well.'

'Prufitt, Prufitt,' said Mitzi, dreamily. 'Of the puddingit is in the eatingit.'

Prufitt had gone when they arrived at the zinc-yard. It seemed to be nearly midnight.

'He's left the list, though,' said Prode. To Mitzi he seemed suddenly vulnerable as concentration, habit, vocation seized him; like a boy frowning over his homework, as he muttered 'One gross bright clouts. H'm. Japanned tee hinges, angle ridges and half-round ditto, h'm. Bull-nose Red Quarry tiles. H'm. Two hundred horizontal S trap left and back inlets . . .'

'Darling, it's like Chaos. Like the mind of God before Creation. All these shapes, half-formed. Calling out for a shaper. What are *these*?'

18

'H'm? Oh, those. Six-inch channel junctions.'

'And these?'

'GLC offsets, junctions, and single and double branches.'

'And these?'

'They're called bright bends. Look, Mitzi Bitzi, don't interrupt. I'll be through in a minute, and then we can—'

'I absolutely must redesign your bright bend. The proportions are wrong. Is there any paper in that little hut?'

'Look, don't force me to say this. Nobody *sees* bright bends. They're part of the drains.'

'*My* bright bends will be seen. We'll have the drains revealed, under thick Perspex covers, with indirect lighting. If it's a *machine à habiter*, let's *see* the machine.'

Prode straightened from checking a carton of hemp, sulphur candles, iron cement, plumbers' black and templars' graphite. He said flatly 'Things are the way they are. You can't design them further. On an asbestos roofing contract, I ask for Plain Wing Ridge, Louvre Blades S Type, Z Type, Apron Flashing Pieces, Soaker Flanges, Dead Lights, Adjustable Nonserrated Hip Capping, I know what I'm going to get. These things are practical, they couldn't be any other way. The words mean what they say. You can't monkey around with Soaker Flanges, there's only one shape they *could* be. All that design! It's for rich daughters, like piano-playing. Building is engineering. We leave a straight wall, maybe you can design some curvy sculpture to go on it if you like; but that's all.'

I've never spelt it out like that before, he thought wonderingly. God, how the heart betrays us! We only show our full selves to those we love, we flaunt what can't be assimilated, instead of keeping in a safe happy garden of platitudes.

Her shoulders shook over the drawing pad. 'Mitz,' he murmured behind her, 'I'm lonely too.'

Through wondrous tears she looked up at him. 'It's for ever, Prode.' She showed him the drawing. 'But if the Design Centre doesn't take this Apron Flashing Piece, I'll *emigrate*.'

To give? To leap in the dark? And to abandon what he had made? The words 'I think you should start on these double-union stopcocks' formed themselves; decisive, Rubicon words, life-changing words formed in his mind. With an immense effort he realised he had not uttered them. He went over to the pile of stop-cocks, multifariously gleaming; a meaningless bright jumble, like life till now. Suddenly he picked one up and took it to the hut.

It was empty. Mitzi had gone.

Life went on. Supplies. Prices. Tenders. Contracts. Forward quotations. Expansion. PRODE, household name. But in brickstock, pipestack, woodpile, zinc-yard, the old joy in these, his *things*, was gone. He worked like a madman.

'Cor, Mr Prode!' (it was Prufitt speaking out of the mist of pain) 'I never see anyone work like you. I reckon your design is to be the biggest Builders' Sundries-man in London.'

Design! The word brought unbearable memories of

20

a husky voice, of great eyes, a certain fall of hair. She had gone to Austria. He had avoided the Haymarket these six months; but now he knew he must go to the Design Centre, again.

Inside, he was instantly drawn, as though pre-knowing what was there. So objective it was, in its pure, logical statement. All previous blowlamps, with their brass bodies, fussy Victorian flame shields and cumbrous handles doubly attached, seemed irrelevant jokes before this marvel of inevitable purity. The straight, un-cluttered handle formed one line with the streamlined nozzle, a line tangential to the body, giving the composition an urgent upward thrust. It made the spectator long to light it, the flames roaring (with what con-tinuous and efficient song coming from that well-wrought cylinder!) and lift it high, high against some old door, attacking with joy the peeling paint.

For Prode it was subjective too; a clear message, an exquisitely written invitation, a call in a husky voice. Blinded with tears he rushed from the Design Centre, not along the steps of memory, to the Tea Centre, but parallel, on a course, this time of surer happiness; to BEA in Lower Regent Street. To Austria.

◖ Sentiment Doesn't Have to be Treacly

Cherished children, offspring, issue,
Dear descendants! See, I kiss you,
I am not a father that
Pines for tidy house or flat;
Tidiness, my brood, my blessing,
Is what up you're always messing
Though beneath your father's heels
Are bricks and books and things with wheels
That make the unsuspecting pater
An impromptu roller-skater;
Do not fear his heart will harden
When he sees, in *House and Garden*
Some sterile room with here and there
A gaunt, asceptic-looking chair,
This won't make him start regretting
Chaos caused by your begetting—
Where children are, he knows full well,
The place will always look like hell,
　　but... O why the dickens, my chickens,

　　　　　　　　　　is *everything* sticky?

　　　Why do my fingers to furniture

　　　　　　　　　　always adhere?

　　　Why, through instinctively sucking on

　　　　　　　　　　lolly or bickie,

　　　Must you smudge every surface in

　　　　　　　　　　sight with a sugary smear?

　　　Must flushing a cistern or raising, when

　　　　　　　　　　rung, the receiver

Mean wiping with Wettex (a wonderful
                  wiping cloth), Reg'd.?
Why, damme, the *car* is all jammy
                  as well; every lever
All gummy, the wheel and the piping
                  on seats, where they're edged!
If simply a doorhandle now and
                  again were all tacky
Through licking of choccy, or rockie
                  or cakie with jam
Not so inclined would I be to requite
                  with a smackie.
You're lucky, my duckie, the Spocky
                  is there by the pram—
But crikey, look! Spocky as well! Even
                  bookies all sticky!
With greasy, adhesive and glutinous
                  glop all the house
Is lacquered! With licquorice, lollipops,
                  suckable, sicky,
Surfaces smothered! Small shock
                  if I grumble and grouse. . . .

And yet I feel, I don't know why,
When everything is clean and dry
I'll be *bored*. To this I cling—
All buds are sticky in the Spring.

23

¶ The Rake's Progress

Q. What is the best method of raking?

A. Many people make the mistake of raking when the soil is too wet. The best time for raking is when—

Q. But I can't *choose* when I rake. Maybe it's wet, maybe it isn't, but there comes this weekend when I have this chance to rush at the Matto Grosso, as my vegetable bed is known. I want to get the whole thing finished, raking and all, *and* shove the stuff in. Already other people's peas are above the ground, the seed potatoes in my shed are putting out those awful under-worldly blind white feelers, like the ghosts of octopuses. Maybe it will be drier next weekend, but this happens to be the one when we haven't got visitors, are not going for a ride, I am not painting the cot or some door, or singing in the Verdi *Requiem*. You don't need to tell *me* it's harder when the soil is wet. I—

A. It pays to buy a good rake, with a heavy steel tines. The ideal length is—

Q. Why do Answers always begin by laying down ideal conditions? Chaps like us have to rake when we get the chance. It's like the instructions on my lawn ferti-lizer: *choose a day when there is no wind, and rain is likely within 48 hours.* Where do they think my lawn is, on the Air Ministry roof? The day chooses me, not the other way round. But to get back to this raking. Whatever length of rake I use it doesn't help with the basic problem, which is the rocksam and rootsam.

A. What on earth is that?

Q. I'm the one that's supposed to ask the questions, but I'm not surprised that you did; no gardening book seems to have heard of rocksam and rootsam, which is what you have on the surface when you are ready for raking. It is to the weekend gardener what flotsam and jetsam are to the sailor—in the Sargasso Sea. It is an irreducible collection of bricks, stones, lumps of concrete, clods of dank clay matted with roots and fibres, gnarled shapes of bog oak, rusty iron things and, in my case, an inexhaustible quantity of fragments from some very large bluish nineteenth-century tea-set. You've heard of the Beaker Folk. Well, we had the Saucer Folk. Now, should one simply pull at this stuff with the rake, or should one push and pull?

A. A gentle back-and-forth motion will help towards the creation of a fine tilth.

Q. You mean if I do it long enough the rocksam and rootsam will just go away? It's true I've glimpsed other gardeners, over fences or through train windows, raking dreamily up and down, making this tilth. But when I do this I make *more* rocksam and rootsam, it seems to come up from underneath.

A. Raking should of course not be undertaken without a thorough preliminary digging and hoeing.

Q. Don't you suggest *I* haven't prepared the ground, my good man. I've got a splendid machine called a Merry Tiller—a name which suggests that little Schumann piece, or perhaps an earlier English drinking song:—

> To ye miller his milth
> To ye tiller his tilth

25

Come jocund lads and merry
Ho, troll ye cup, etc.
To ye filler his filth
And ye killer his kilth
And eke al care we'll bury
Ho, toss ye pot, etc.

It's dead keen and extremely efficient: it drags me round doing the work of three men and a boy, digging much deeper than the four of us did when we used spades. I can see wonderful merry tilth all over the Matto Grosso; but I can also see rocksam and rootsam, the better you dig the more there is. So maybe I should just *pull* the rake?

A. Large stones should be removed.

Q. Listen, it's not a question of picking up a few 'large stones,' as you call them. Since I can't make the rocksam and rootsam just go away I have to pull it all to one end of the bed, a great intractable heap of rubbish, barrowloads of it every year. It so happens I've got next to my garden an uncultivated bit called (by the mortgage documents, not by me) The Gritches; and since we came here in 1956 I've been building a range of artificial mountains, there's a great nettle-covered bank over 4 ft high right across the end already. People say, Oh, it'll rot down. Don't you believe it, it all rots *up*.

Yet the garden itself is no lower. Where does it all come from? Actually, by the time I've raked it and carted a couple more barrowloads of r. and r. to Mt. Gritch it's getting dark on Sunday evening and too late to put anything in. By the next available weekend enough new weeds have appeared to make a quick run round with the Merry Tiller seem a good idea—*more* r. and r. What do you advise?

A. Wait till they bring out a Merry Raker.

⟨ False Beards in Cleethorpes

◆◆◆◆◆◆◆◆◆◆◆◆◆◆◆◆◆◆◆◆◆◆◆◆◆◆◆◆◆◆◆◆◆◆◆◆◆◆◆

INDUSTRIAL ESPIONAGE is the big thing in the North Sea these days. Every time an oil rig moves half a mile or burns a test flare, there are watchers from rival firms circling round in helicopters and fishing-boats. It seems extraordinary that the spy fiction industry hasn't got on to this yet.

Scene: Room 37402 in the Shell Building. Enter Seamus Condery.
Secretary: How did you get in? The door's locked.
Condery: Melted the bolt with this, dear (*produces what looks like a cigarette lighter from his pocket*). Transistorized laser. Where's the bed? And why is there only one of you?
Secretary: That will be enough of that, Mr Condery. I'm only temporary here, they sent me on loan from Room 15023, in the Tied Garage Division, to help the new Director of Intelligence, Mr—(*there is a soft thud as she slumps over the typewriter. The Director, a bald executive type with dark glasses, is standing in the doorway to the inner office, Room 37402A, holding a blowpipe*).
Director: Only an anaesthetic dart. She'll come round in an hour or so. Come in, Condery. I'd rather she, or anyone else, didn't reveal my name to you yet. I am N.
Condery: What happened to M?
Director (harshly): Failure is not tolerated here, Condery. Two months, and we still don't know whether

28

the Gas Council Consortium's strike is a gas-drive or a depletion-type field. M has been posted to Advertising. Now, take a look at this street plan of Cleethorpes ...

* * *

Scene 2: *A scruffy bed-sitting room in St Edwin's Guest House, Station Road, Cleethorpes. Lomas Watercress, a seedy, anxious, bungling man in his forties, with three days' beard, is at a telescope pointing through a small gap in the lace curtains. Suddenly he stiffens, mumbles into the mike of a hidden transmitter.*
Watercress: Aramco No. 2 on flare. (*The door opens softly and a beautiful girl in a shiny black plastic mackintosh enters. Watercress whirls round, pulling out a gun, but it sticks in his trouser pocket.*) Ah, Heidi, liebchen, it's you. You gave me a fright.
Heidi: Lo, you're hopeless (*looks through telescope*). You're on to Grimsby Gasworks. (*Swings telescope round*). *There's* Aramco. They're still drilling. Down to 4,000, with a whip-stock deviation of 12 degrees.
Watercress (jealously): You've been drinking with your 'copter pilot!
Heidi: So? What would he do to me if he found I was telling you, and you were telling Union Schweinische A.G.? What would Shell say? What would your Mr Harold Wilson say?
Watercress (burying head in hands): Forgive me, Liebchen. You know they promised to get my brother back across the Curtain.
Heidi: I passed your landlady on the way up. She said

to ask if you want cod and chips or toad-in-the-hole for supper.

Watercress: I'll fix us an omelette up here. We'll put the Bartok on, and after—

Heidi: No, I must go. (*She has seen a car pull up outside*).

* * *

Scene 3. *The Jolly Joybar and Bingo Lounge of a Skegness holiday camp. Mingling among the bingo players and redcoats are oil technologists, helicopter pilots, geologists, fishermen and special agents from a dozen countries. Heidi, drinking with a silent Korean, starts when Condery, in a sharkskin dinner-jacket, enters: but she has recovered her poise when he saunters up to them at the bar.*

Condery: Nice little torture room they've got on Constellation. But they reckoned without my little laser and this (*indicating frogman suit under dinner jacket*). So. I've booked a double at the Commercial Arms in Wainfleet. Take your choice, honey. Either you come or I tell the Gas Council all. (*The Korean makes a lightning chop but Condery forestalls him and he falls inert*). It's a form of Greek wrestling called Korote. Picked it up in the part of Asia Minor that used to be called Caria. There's a groove in the fibula just below the knee where the lateral popliteal nerve passes close to the bone. Carian korote. Better than Korean karate, eh?

Bingo caller (winking): All the sixes. Kelly's Eye. Kelly, aye, yay, yay. (*Condery rushes out, almost knocking over*

Watercress, whose eyes are gleaming behind his glasses).
Watercress: I say, I got your note. And I know what a kelly is, too, it's hexagonal bit that drives the drill. I say, do you think that was a signal? I—(*several men in leather jackets have also rushed out and there is an immense noise as five helicopters start up outside. When Watercress and Heidi manage to get out through the crush they are just in time to see Condery waving down sardonically at them from the passenger seat, illuminated by the glow of an immense flare out at sea).*
Watercress: What's the use? I haven't *got* a helicopter. Only a bicycle.
Heidi: Nor will he have in a minute. I made a hole in his petrol tank. Come on.
Watercress: Where to?
Heidi: Wainfleet, The Commercial Arms.

❡ Another B.A. Bites the Dust

●◆◆●

DR SEPTIMUS COURTLY peered over his pince-nez at the other members of Redundant Arts Graduates for Business and Government. 'Well, gentlemen, a successful afternoon! We've placed them all, even that boy who did so well in Sumerian and Akkadian. These new giant trawlers are a promising field.'

'Shouldn't bank on it,' grunted Sir Joel Hardbody, the industrial member. 'There won't be many of 'em, at half a million pounds each; and we were lucky they didn't want a qualified chap to run their library.'

'Dear me, yes, everything is so specialized nowadays, even advertising, and the men do so hate starting as trainees. Still, that's the function of RAGBAG, isn't it, to keep one step ahead of the specializing trend and permeate industry with true arts men? You'll just let us see the list before you send it off to Lord Snow, Mr Secretary?'

'*Haud omnes ad laborem direximus,*' said the secretary. '*Manet casus difficillimus—*'

'Er, if you don't mind, Mr Trefusis,' said Dr Courtly, looking apprehensively at Hardbody and the psychiatrist Peter Pragma, 'I don't think our, er, industrial and psychiatric colleagues have quite, er, kept up their Latin. If you could, er—'

'Sorry, gentlemen,' said Trefusis, with a barely visible smile, 'A *lapsus linguae*, I was only saying that we haven't found jobs for them all, there's still one very difficult case. This boy Freshkin, 2nd class honours

32

in Romance languages, 2nd fifteen at school, 2nd son of 2nd marriage. Tendency to parontia.'

'Goodness Pragma, what jargon you fellows talk,' said Dr Courtly, 'What on earth is parontia?'

'I may not talk dog-Latin,' said Pragma rather stiffly (for he had more or less discovered parontia, which was often referred to as Pragma's Syndrome), 'but your Greek should tell you that it means a standing outside being. It is to the existential norm what the manic-depressive cycle is to the emotional one. A parontic alternates between an intense feeling for the reality of the world coupled with a soaring confidence, and a dreamlike sense that all facts are illusory. It is common among arts graduates. I should recommend some industry where the machinery has some very real and visible function, so that fantasy-withdrawal is held in check. . . .'

Thus it was that some weeks later Slingsby Freshkin found himself in the rough wooden hut that served as the mobile head office of Grogg Earth Moving. Big Jim Grogg, on the telephone, motioned him to sit down with a wave of a huge paw.

'. . . O.K., Bull, get the lads on to it with the two big graders. And I want those culverts done down to 28 by Friday.' He put the phone down. 'Freshkin, Freshkin? Ah, you're the one Hardbody wrote about. We do a lot of jobs for him.' He peered at the letter. 'Romance languages, what's that? You write love stories, kid? No, don't explain. I left school at 14, built this thing up from one little ole lorry, but I don't hold it against you, see?'

'I remember we had another kid from Hardbody once, he started to tell me what he'd learnt, it was all about some monster in a poem called Bee-Wolf. Imagine a bee-wolf! He overturned a Thwaites Dumper the second day. So you better be my personal assistant, help with the papers and stuff. Look, here are the P.A.Y.E. scales and the overtime dockets for Bull O'Riordan's lot; just make out his credit slips and bring them to us at Bridge 43. Take the Land Rover.' They were building a motorway.

Alone in the office, Freshkin stared at the meaningless phrases. *Proportional excess not deducted unless pro rata schedules are aggregated* ... the grand student dreams, the wonderful absorption of the mind, it had all come to this, these papers, this table, this awful sense of insufficiency combined with boredom. ...

'What's the trouble, lad?' It was Mr Edwards, the kindly old Clerk of Works, with five pens in his breast pocket. Mistaking Freshkin's dreaminess for concentration, he expertly totted up the slips, leaving the boy far behind with his rapid explanations. 'You'll soon learn, lad.'

Outside, the busy sunlit scene, huge mounds, swarming men, like a Breughel painting of some vast medieval activity except for the enormous roaring yellow machines, swung Freshkin's mood the other way. Hair streaming in the wind, he roared up the empty motorway singing a Limousin folk song. *Del vostre bon advertiment, amor mueve la terra,* he sang; love moves the earth. He stopped by the biggest yellow machine of all. There was no one about. I can do anything, he

34

thought; I'll show them. He got out of the Land Rover and climbed into the monster's cab. Good, that was the starter button. Now, which of these seven levers make it move? A long hydraulic arm lurched into the air. No, try this one then. A frightful grinding noise. This one—help, going round in a circle. This one. Ah —no, climbing up the bank. Can't stop it. . . .

Freshkin was miraculously unhurt when Grogg and O'Riordan rushed up to the machine, lying on its side and waving a huge skip in the air like a wounded wasp—

Or could there be some other explanation for the following advertisement, which was in *The Times* on June 5th:—

WANTED—ARTS GRADUATE

with a strong sense of fact and not over-confident, to act as personal assistant to Managing Director of substantial excavation business.

◆◆◆◆◆◆◆◆◆◆◆◆◆◆◆◆◆◆◆◆◆◆◆◆◆◆◆◆◆◆◆◆◆◆◆◆◆◆◆

"SOOKY, £11/10; Beooy Betab Elpykelpet,
£5/10; Oozab, £10/10; Lyfoo, £6; Pegoo,
£12/10; Ceyoo, £5; Etini, 25/-; Eloop, 50/-;
Rosalrwhoo, 65/-; Sgyoo, £4; 7.3 cm. Hektor
f. 1.9., £15; Robot Junior body, £16; Robot
Universal viewfinder, £12/10."

—small ad. in Amateur Photographer.

Spooky ad, no fooly (*lyfoo*, yoo see? Lyfoo, fooly;
samey letter, jiggle a bit to helpit). Oozad vokab lyk soo
in ad, oo speltit soo? Oo talkit sooch a spooky ingroopy
bit, cool and perky with wordbits inscrootab–*elpykelpet,
beooy, betab*? What betooken? Joken or loopy? Noonoo
no. Oozit paygoo money for jest or kooky ad? Noo, noone
so moony! Must be meaning in gobbledygoo, *etini*
meanee somting, *eloop* is soomting of beooty and clear
to soomoon oo readit, to clood-up ingrooper. But oo?

Pooh and phooey, yoo say? Nooting obscoor in jerky-
wordy ad, any fooly cansee it all habdoo with camera,
fokal optik and stoof in camera shoop, it simply an ad
to sellkit sooch as *eloop* and *etini* and soochlyk proops.
If anybob knoo the roops, not get loozad or loost in
camera world, here are scoops in ad—quick, put on
snood and booties, shooty off on scooter to camera
shoop, swoopygrab for loot; looky; looky, oo could
hoop to get *eloop* for 50 boob, it's a beooty, a snipini!
Betab bargain, off the *pegoo*! It's hooty, man!

But doonty say *pooh* and *phooey* in sooch a snooty
way! Not stoopid to whistle (*rosolrwhoo! rosol-*

rwhoo! Like purselip owl nootbird rustly whittawhoo in dusky groove!) in wonder at pidgini jingle of jargony ad. Not soo, no stoopid! Scrootini mysoo in camera shoop, not fooly me! Nevar I cine lens or camera boody or develpyselfkit with sooch a scroowy list of word I niver hear spooken, lyk *oozab, elpykelpet, sgyoo.*

Can't fooly me, I knoo trooly words of ooverseas footygraphkit—rollei, nikon, ikonta, leica, pentax, kodak. Hoo, yoo, all tricky fokal tackle and optik von jena und zeiss I knoo, osaka nagashahi tripods I cognise and covet in windooshoopy. Mysoo lookini windoo at camera shoop, glood to windoo with loonchtym groop of phootodab windooshoopers, rooful ikontafford it. But daydroom, droom of affloo, sooper-ikonta teknik in smoothy troo leather casini! De looxy imago reflex of my daydroom—looky, boodl and loocre accrood, or scoopy the pooly (hurroo, yarroo!), I swoop (oo soo grandi!) into camera shoop, say all hooty and snooty to shooplad or coonterbeooy, 'Shoo me your booty; I leica beicamera with cooplefinder, corekted für parallax, pentax, soopertax.'

And shooman dandini boow and scroopy, kiss me booty! 'Certini sir! You want yashimatic or handi oooperat? Stepini shooroom. Here is noovel mini with televoo and scroo-fit interchangeab adjoostab infini, corektor biltini floosh and flashpoop; a really snoopy! Sootab for booth kind of work in polyfooto dooty—the stoodyoo groopy, pinoopy beooty posini bikini, or scoopy shooty for noospap. Oo, a snoop!'

But heu! Boobini camera shoop, fooly freely to ask for *sooky, oozab, etini* and soochlyk. Shoopman smirkini soopyrior, winki to ingroopmen, the chosen feoow, hooty laughter to rafter—oozit loopyman ask for *pegoo, sygoo,* drooly boobytalk? 'Yoo are mistooky, sir; no *betab* in this estab, noo *eloop* for 50 boob! Oonly pantex, ilfoo, agfo, yoo can ceyoo yooself in shoocase bei ikonter!'

Doomy daydroom! Doom me to roost on ootside of ingroop, niver a cloo to groovy ad but load of heooy—soo:—

Etini, Italian smoothy *beooy,* looky in Robot universal viewfinder, see in bikini junior body of *Pegoo,* cooleen from Dooblin (begob, bedad, *betab*!), woolfy whistle *rosolrwhoo.* Can't elpyselfet! Long to scoopini arms and floo away. But hoo? Also in viewfinder, oo but *Hektor,* beooy-friend of Pegoo, beootyfool muscle but stoopid! Scoop! Askini to tea—*lyfoo* tea from Chini—shoo etchini to Pegoo and say '*Eloop* with me, I'll make yoo my cooky by hooky or crooky!' Poor Pegoo, too latey see what meanee Etini.

But Hektor tumble to roose, hotfooty to Villa Etini, boomp thoomp on vilaini door. 'Oozab bangin?' she say, new hoop in heart. 'My Hektor protektor! Whoopy!' Breakini door and bam! Boom! Boop! Aaaaghoo *Sgyoo*! Gloop! Groogh! Etini fini and scoot . . .

Hoo, could shooty on cine, glamoury camera scoopy, ingroop after all. I've seeni loopier.

HOME

ℭ Hornets Anonymous

◆◆◆◆◆◆◆◆◆◆◆◆◆◆◆◆◆◆◆◆◆◆◆◆◆◆◆◆◆◆◆◆◆◆◆◆

THERE ARE hornets zooming about our house already, in their evil, absentminded way, as if looking at us with one eye and saying 'just don't make us notice you, that's all.' They seem part of the portent of a weird, rainless, windless spring. Hornets, in March and April!

(Is England changing, what happened to the great Dickens winter, the real cold and rain? What dragons and moaning female figures with comet-trailing hair will appear in the unnatural summer sky—where the atheist God lives—while we sit uneasy in the dry garden, warmer than in real June, and the birds sing hysterically in bare black trees, as though it were an eclipse in reverse? Where is the English rain? If this is spring, when torrid summer comes will Ipswich be a shimmering mirage in a desert, will skulls gleam in the hot sand outside the oasis of Bou Rnem Outh, will El Tham be the hottest and driest place in the world and Birmi Ngham a sinister settlement in the up-country tropical Ar Den forests?)

We have had these hornets for years, but only in July and August and then only at night, when they have sent probing parties of suicide scouts to try to shoot out the lights; groaning and zumbling round the shades at low speeds clearly awkward for them, easy targets for our Aerosol flak. It says in my encyclopaedia 'the predominant colour is red, with some yellow on head, abdomen and wings. The colonies include not more than 200 individuals and nest in hollow trees and other sheltered places.' These individuals are yellow, but they're twice as big as any wasp I've ever seen and the official pest man said they were hornets. (He said he could only help when I had located the nest). It's my guess they've been painting each other yellow during the long waits in the ops room.

How to find out where the perishers live? Until this year I really believed this hollow tree stuff, I was convinced they lurked in a field facing us (they seemed to hang about the front door more than the back). On July and August nights, wearing rubber boots gloves and a hat trimmed with an all-round veil of old net curtain, like a lunatic morris dancer, I would go tromping about shining a torch, poised for instant flight, kicking old logs.

But now, this strange, warm spring, there is escalation. They appear for the first time in broad daylight, and always in the bedroom nearest the hatch to the only part of the roof that can be entered by a human being. Yes, they *are* yellow. Can they be just very fat wasps, gorged from eating a whole hollow tree, moving now to eat my roof?

'That's a hornet if ever I saw one,' says my friend Harblow, who tends to turn up at fine weekends, and has probably never seen a hornet. His desire to use the smoke canister left by the assistant pest man has overcome his fear of all hymenoptera (I get too angry with their devious and wandering hostility to be afraid).

'But first we'll shove a light up there and see if we

can spot where they're coming from to it.' He rigs up
a long flex on a bedside lamp. I am quite ready to nip
up the step-ladder and put it in the roof, but Harblow
says we might as well protect ourselves from the start
in case the light maddens them.

We go downstairs to get gloves and the hat-curtain
thing. 'If we were both under this we could face opposite ways and have all-round vision.' He puts another
hat under it. It looks like some bridal garment for a
Siamese twin.

There is just room for both our heads and shoulders
through the hatch. The light reveals a floor of solid but
sagging boards, pipes lagged with huge old tablecloths,
enormous cobwebs or—horror! Is that black thing above
us crawling with—no, it's a cobweb too.

Something is going *zzz*. I see it first, a hornet walking
across the boards straight towards the light. It keeps
falling on one side, as though it were wounded but de-
termined to throw a grenade. Harblow rapidly dis-
appears down the ladder, I have a spare hat. The hornet
is coming from the far corner, where I can just make out
a round shape that might be a nest ('about the size of a
football,' said the pest man) or just a lump of plaster.
The trouble is, if you point a bedside lamp at anything
the light from the open end of the shade dazzles you.

We light the canister and retire immediately. Next
day the walking hornet is dead in its tracks anyway;
they must be down to 190 by now. The pest man comes.
'That's no good,' he says. 'It needs the big cylinder,
nozzle right in the mouth of the nest. Stirs 'em up a
bit. Tricky in a confined space. If that *is* the nest . . .'

'Why not do it from outside?' says Harblow. 'Up a ladder, get a few slates off. Just the weather for it.'

But the pest man knows, and I know, it's not the right weather at all.

❡ Interior, with Birds

THERE IS a whiff of something primal, terrible,
about a wild bird discovered in the living-room. Not in
in the obvious sense that it might attack, like the ones
in the Hitchcock film (some ancestral fear for the eyes;
who says they go for the eyes?); you just try that in
here, mate, I think as it hops about under the piano;
you're only this bird and I'm a man. It stares at me with
eyes utterly incapable of showing anything, even fear.

It *acts* fear all right, although I keep saying *come on
then* in an idiotically dulcet voice. Some crazy life force
jerks it away from me. Life ought to go with some kind
of personality, however rudimentary; and this thing that
squawks and flutters and escapes from my hand where
it quivers with dreadful membranes, making me lurch
after it and bang my head on the underside of the piano,
is no kind of person at all. There just isn't a bird-person
the way there is a cat-person or even a tortoise-person.
It's just this mad quantum of life haphazardly lodged
in a flimsy mechanism of feathers and brittle bone.

Birds are all right outside, in crowds (maybe there's
no such thing as one bird), they skimble and twitter,
they flute and carol in trees, their darting feathers gave
us the idea for the still plumes of angels, who compre-
hend the whole scheme instantaneously. But this live
contraption under my piano—a blackbird usually, which
makes it even weirder, a faultless, mindless prima donna
—belongs to no possible scheme, life has darted at random into this airborne musical box as capriciously as

43

it does into families, empires, civilizations, and may as capriciously withdraw. 'Corm on yer little perisher, do stop beating at the only window that doesn't open, and leave us to our human order in this room. . . .'

Really, of course, the only thing to do is leave all the windows open and go away, and sooner or later it will get out by accident, thinking God knows what to itself (that was a hell of a funny tree I was in, or, what was that solid air they had in squares? or what a great clumsy ass that was under the piano, or more likely, akkakrrabbabbl, or just '   '). But last time we couldn't do this because rain was driving straight at the windows. It was a sparrow this time (they can't even sing, what are *they* for?), the whole thing was like that bit about the conversion of Northumbria, by the Venerable Bede, where man's life is compared to a sparrow coming for a brief moment out of the winter storms into a lighted feasting hall. Also, Harblow was staying with us, and we needed the living-room to live in.

'How did it get in, then?' said Harblow triumphantly. As if anyone ever sees a bird actually come in. They are always discovered there when you come in. It's no good being logical about birds.

He crawled under the piano. 'Tum on den,' he said. 'Tum on, birdie. Tum to—blast it!' He crawled out, rubbing his head. The sparrow flew up to a picture and dropped its sixth dropping.

It is a long time since we were at the OCTU but it has left Harblow with a permanent instinct to treat anything like this in the same way as one of those group tasks, like getting a ton weight over a river or rescuing a

44

wounded man from a tree, which one always took over from the previous cadet when the weight was right in the river or the cadet playing the wounded man was suspended by a rope round his ankle 40 feet above the ground. Someone, somewhere, is giving marks for logic and coolness.

'Don't let it go up the chimney,' he said. 'I've got an idea. Back in a second.' I half expected him to re-appear with a cage and some pan pipes, singing *Fo-hor I'M the jo-holly-y BIRD ca-hatch-ER*, or dressed in some kind of Chaucerian wildfowling costume with a flat hat and a lot of nets. What he actually came in with was a saucer of bread and milk, a large plastic basket that we put washing in, and some string. The sparrow went back under the piano.

'You don't seem to have any seed,' he said, 'but I daresay they like bread and milk.' Over the saucer he balanced the basket so that a slight pull on the string would bring it down.

'I'll just pop outside. Open the window a fraction and pass me the string. It won't do it while we're here.' I did as he asked and followed him into the rain, since it seemed the only thing to do. I bet the Venerable Bede never thought of men outside and birds inside.

It rained down our necks, but to my astonishment the bird did go to the saucer. Harblow pulled the string. No wonder he was a Captain and I wasn't. 'Now all we need is a board to slide underneath and then we'll bring the whole thing outside,' he said.

After a lot of rummaging in the shed and cursing among useless little derelict bicycles we found a piece of plywood two feet square (actually we broke up a crate full of moss and old dolls). We went back to the living-room with it. The bird instantly flew out of the basket with perfect ease, since the holes were too big, and into the kitchen.

'What about those nets you have in the shed? If we stretched some between two poles the height of the room we could each take one and close in on a corner. There isn't much furniture here. We could move—'

But the kitchen window was on the leeward side, and anyway there were no best curtains to get wet here. I opened it and we went away. So, as far as I could tell, did the sparrow.

❡ The Fencer Foiled

◆◆◆

THERE IS something marvellously unscientific about most routine parental activity. We are forever doing things which we know to be useless but which are somehow not merely hopeless. Most cooking for children, for instance, is done in the sure knowledge that they won't like it. They play about trying to cut imaginary fat off the matchhead-sized nodules of meat in mince which they have praised extravagantly in someone else's house and which has been carefully bought from the same butcher. They reject subtle puddings made with milk and eggs for awful pink glop made by adding cold water to some hideous plastic powder. What they would really like is not three meals a day but a piece of dry bread every half hour, some raisins, the outsides of seven apples, and a pound of chocolate biscuits. Nevertheless, mothers continue to cook.

It is when these parental actions also call for a technical skill one hasn't got that one really sees how unscientific they are. For instance, every time one of my children reaches 18 months and becomes drunk with mobility, I have to start making another fence to keep it in.

In the present case, buried in long grass and nettles are the ruins of four previous hopeless fences. Basically, they are made of wire netting and wooden posts. But anyone who has ever tried this will know it's not possible, because the top of wire netting is always longer than the bottom, or the other way round, and you cannot get it taut.

Doubtless there are professional tools, although I don't believe professionals would look at a job like this. They only make fences in the open, as it were, and in straight lines. My fences have to go through gloomy thickets and semi-hedges. (The laurel is a bush, but we have laurel *trees*). The unkempt edges of the area I'm trying to fence look enclosed enough; but of course the wilder, more overgrown and inaccessible to an adult the place is, the more it attracts the tiny escapists.

I thus find myself doing what no professional fence-maker ever has to attempt—knocking a bluntly pointed piece of chestnut paling into ground full of tangled roots with the back of a great axe (I've got an axe and I'm damned if I'm going to buy a mallet just for this one job). Half the time a proper blow cannot be delivered because some branch in the gloomy thicket impedes the upswing. The axe is really too heavy for one-hand use, but the first 30 or 40 blows have to be so, because my left hand is holding the post. When the thing will finally stand, I climb on a chair to get height for the real pile-driving, and the post topples gently over just as the axe comes whistling down, either chipping a piece off the top or missing altogether and dealing the crosspiece of the chair a terrible blow.

Later, under the rain of blows from a weapon with too small a point of impact, the post splits, or at any rate gets to the point where the next blow will split it, and half an hour is now spent in finding wire to bind it. The posts of my finished (if that is the word) fence have a topnotch effect where repeated bashing has driven the wood over the containing wire.

It's not only that professionals would have proper mallets; they would have magic. Once, two elderly gnomes came to fit the carpet in our long, thin drawing-room. It stood in a roll over three feet high, reaching across the width of the room, from which all the furniture had been removed except a grand piano (well, a boudoir grand; but it is well known that the molecular weight of pianos is higher than that of plutonium). I watched these men. They had special hammers, special tacks and, above all, special kneelers with spikes underneath and a padded sticking-up bit which they banged in a special way with their special knees, so that the spikes gripped the carpet and stretched it.

But they also had magic. How would they get the huge roll past the piano, which no two men could possibly lift bodily? I went out for less than two minutes to get them a cup of tea, and when I came back there was the piano on the laid side of the carpet, the roll still a foot high, and they were banging away unconcernedly.

Well, there are probably special hammers, special geared wrenches for pulling wire netting taut, special men with three hands—one to hold the netting tight, one to hold the fool staple straight before a momentary relaxation of one's straining hold jerks it out, and one for the hammer. There are probably all kinds of magic. But the resulting fence wouldn't keep the child in.

And mine has, even though it's full of holes.

❡ Giving up Sailing

I DON'T THINK I have quite given it up yet, but summer by summer, slowly, painfully, I am wrenching myself away from the fantasy of being a sailor.

I don't mean a man in a funny hat doing a hornpipe; I mean, of course, a man owning a nice little twenty-foot yawl (would it be? Or ketch? Or sloop? I could draw it, in my mind's eye I know what it looks like); conversant with tides, skilled in that ultimate ability to do the last twenty yards up to a mooring against a strong wind; able to write this sort of thing—'so we made a hurried change of sail, from genoa to No. 1 jib. The Rolling Grounds, the Pitching Grounds, and then into the quieter waters of Harwich Estuary by the Beach End buoy....'

Hammond Innes wrote that, and I live even nearer to Harwich Estuary than he does. For years now I've been saying 'Well, it's wonderfully convenient living near these estuaries (there's the Blackwater, and the Orwell and the Deben, as well as the Stour), because I want my children to grow up knowing how to sail a boat.' It is true that the eldest has already learnt something; but not from me. She's been on a course. I'm the one that hasn't been on a course, and what I am giving up is the fantasy that I ever shall. (Where are there courses for men of forty-six, never mind about girls of eleven? It's like these grants one keeps reading about 'for young writers' so that they can live on some Mediterranean island and write another novel. Gosh, if I were a young writer I could do that without a grant. We middle-aged writers, we're the chaps who need grants, to help with the school fees—and children's sailing courses—let alone getting to Mediterranean islands).

If I ever get to sail now it will be the children who teach me. I must abandon this picture, lived with for so long, of this ketch (or yawl), my wife handing up a steaming mug of coffee from the galley as we round Outer Gabbard, Barrow Deep and Galloper (lightships; thank you, Hammond Innes) in a pearly dawn; maybe on our way *back* from a Mediterranean island.

The trouble is that like all dreams it has a touch of eternity, something unassailable, some hint of paradise. That mixture of adventurous joy with wide peace that you have in the ideal sailing dream has as much to do with heaven as with any actual sea or boat. In any actual sailing I have done, as crew in someone else's boat, there has been a strongly unparadisal air of anti-climax, largely due to the realization that this is no more the dream of sailing than turning over the music for someone is being a pianist.

Yet there are so many sailing men. And these men, quite ordinary on land, have, when you are in their boat, an effortless superiority. There is something about the way they utter those formal cries, *ready about!* or *gybe-oh!*, something about their narrowed eyes, about the way they don't have so much time to talk as you do, about the feeling that in the last resort your very life is now dependent on their skill, that gives a moral quality to their superiority. They were more, well, more dedicated than you, they didn't just dream about it.

How the hell do they do it? I can understand when it's Hammond Innes, he writes best-sellers. But most people who manage to do all this sailing don't write at all, let alone best-sellers. It's not so much the money, it's the time they seem to have. They must all be in jobs where every Friday afternoon they can rub their hands at 5.30 or even 5, and say 'Well, that's it until 9' (or 9.30) 'on Monday,' and absolutely all that time is free for them to drive down to their estuary, do all their caulking and baling and splicing and painting and chandling on Friday evening, and still have two whole days on the water. On my last Saturday, a not untypical one, I was still sitting in my study at 7 p.m. trying to find a rhyme for 'oblige' (there isn't one).

Of course they too must have wives, lawns, speech days, churches, week-end guests, joint shopping missions, dogs, books, letters, pianos, measles, children's parties, banks, hairdressers, cats, painting jobs, children's bicycle punctures, untidy sheds, other children, and similar time-consumers, like the rest of us. But such is their single-mindedness, their power of organization, that they still have these huge calm areas of time which they can fill with the graceful and relaxed arabesques of sailing, beautiful curved and organic motions among infinite waters and pure winds, refreshing the soul.

Sometimes, when they are towing their boats down to the estuary, I pass them in my car; it is five years old but their cars are older, and I think I have a glimpse of their dedication—maybe they don't care about having a smart new car (as mine, unbelievably, was so recently), they don't throw their money about in this ostentatious way, any honest old thing will do that will get their boat down to the water. And then I have doubts, possibly that is just their boat-towing car, they have another, beautifully new car back in the garage.

At other times I try to console myself with the thought that sailing is a hobby exclusive of all others. After all, I sing. I sing in local groups and in London. But when I come to think of it, the man who sits next to me at the New Philharmonic Chorus rehearsals (which sometimes seem to me to be on every night of the week) has a boat of his own. It wouldn't surprise me if they all had, maybe we could have a regatta and races with the Bach Choir on the Solent.

No, people who sail have some secret which has eluded me, and I might as well admit it. Before I finally decided to give up my sailing-fantasy—i.e., only last summer—I bought a book called *Sailing and Seamanship* by Eric Howells. It was the most practical-looking of the whole row of sailing books in the shop, and if I knew it all I am sure I should not only be able to take up moorings against the wind but right a capsize (helmsman clambers on to upturned side while crew goes into the water to windward and steps on to the centreboard), and I should know what sound-signals to make in thick weather on a vessel at anchor. (Ring bell vigorously for five seconds. If vessel is over three hundred and fifty feet long, in addition beat gong at stern. Who would have thought it, a gong?) And I see from one glance at page seventeen that my ideal boat is a sloop. A yawl has a second mast right aft, a ketch has a second mast nearer amidships. . . .

What really depresses me is seeing that Mr Howells is headmaster of Melton Constable Secondary Modern School, and Commander B. Lucke, who edited this admirable book, is Head of the Department of Navigation, Sir Anthony Deane County Secondary School, Dovercourt, Harwich. There just wasn't a Department of Navigation in any school I was at. How am I going to get away from moorings, let alone take them up again, without crashing into the rows of neatly moored sloops, cat-boats, yawls, ketches, etc., belonging to all these kids, who can answer questions like these tests at the back of the book? Where would you recommend a helmsman to sit when running goose-winged? Describe how you would execute a controlled gybe (say something sarcastic without moving a muscle?). Explain and illustrate what is meant by the 'Orange Pip Theory' of how a boat sails. What do you understand by Worming, Parcelling and Serving a Rope? Alas, nothing. It's too late now.

But perhaps, if I ever write a best-seller, I will have this sloop, which I have learned to sail at a special course for one man, and I shall have the time because all the caulking and chandling will be done by this ex-Chief Petty Officer. He will have everything ready when we go down to the estuary.

'Evening, Ben,' I shall say.

'Evening to you,' he will say in his blunt way. 'She's all shipshape. I've fitted the Wykeham Martin and the new pintles, and I've parcelled the long splice on the main halyard for you.' He gazes across the harbour bar. 'Tide's taking off. Neaps tomorrow. Reckon you'll be off now to catch the ebb.'

'Time for a drink first, Ben.' We all go into this very clean, bare, white pub. 'Ha, thought you'd be out past Barrow Deep by now,' says the landlord.

'Oh, we're only trying out the Wykeham Martin this time,' I reply. 'The usual, Ben?' The other people in the pub are jolly laughing sailing people, not the dour kind. As we drink, a wide twilight peace descends imperceptibly on the estuary, riding lights begin to twinkle across the calm water. Won't do to stay here too long, we shall never get away. . . .

Of course we shan't. I've given it up.

ABROAD

❡ The Last Train to St Petersburg

ALL REAL travel is in the mind. No actual foreign
place is as other as you think it's going to be; that
follows from the mere fact of your being there, the
same old you.

You stand and stare at the Skolt Lapps rounding up
reindeer, at the towers of Manhattan, or the lamasery of
Shekar-Dzong, in your English trousers; but you don't
live here, it's really nothing to do with you. Soon you'll
be putting a latchkey into some boring old British front
door again. At the actual time of seeing marvels a dis-
appointed little voice somewhere inside you says *Why
isn't this changing me?*

But nothing can shatter the illusion of timetables.
Their mere lists of names are poetic enough, in the strict
Mallarméan sense. Mallarmé wrote: 'I say, a flower;
and ... musically there arises an idea itself more frag-
rant, the one absent from all bouquets.' There is a list
incised in stone, in the walls of Blackfriars Station, of
station names with a fragrance absent from all actual
stations; Darmstadt, Geneva, Florence, St Petersburg.
One has only to cross the road, go up the clomping
stairs, ask for a single to St Petersburg at the little
window, and one is perhaps, on the very same fatal
and passionate line where Anna Karenina stumbled beside the track and wished for death. . . .

But timetables are better than mere lists of names,

the raw material of dreams. At their best they supply not only the content of dreams but the form as well, they propose actual journeys. Like all great Romantic Art they are essentially a product of the nineteenth century, when public transport—above all the railway, the steam railway—had at last become a reality, making Travel for Travel's Sake just as possible as Art for Art's.

Just as Shakespeare lived at a time when the English language was shining and new, when Medieval met Renaissance, so does your true nineteenth-century time-table recall that Springtime when all those lakeside hotels—Bristol, Bellevue, Palace—were brand new; when it really was wonderful to leave the centre of London at 10.20 a.m. and be in the centre of Paris at 4.20 p.m., as you could in 1863 (not that it's much quicker even by air, today). The packed columns of train-times seem, on these yellowed pages, to strike a perfect balance between necessary travel (for commerce or pilgrimage, such as men had always known) and the new travel-as-expression, still personal, not yet a mass-movement.

If I taught literature I would make something like the *Livret Chaix, Guide Officiel des Voyageurs,* 1863 edition, a set book. I would make my students do weekly essays from it. What was the gold coinage of Venice, I might ask:

1 scudo	3	ozellas
1 ozella	4	zecchini
1 zecchino	14	lire

The first Italian Parliament had already met at Turin,

but in Venice, still under the Austrians, what cloaked figures muttering under dim arches, what beautiful woman signalling by a raised eyebrow under the glittering chandeliers in an old palace—and what payment in hard currency (a scudo was worth over £5)? And then away, leaving Venice comfortably at 11 a.m. Mestre 11.23. Mogliano 11.39; and as the train draws into Preganziol (11.48), a solitary figure, dressed in black, on the country platform. The pair are in Vienna at 5.25 p.m. From there they can go anywhere; Pryzworsk (p. 357), or Czegled, Szegedin, Temesvar and Basiasch (p. 358).

In dozens of sparkling new cast-iron termini, the railways have brought a delightful unity to the whole of Europe and Russia (prematurely, we now see, gazing sadly through the iron curtains of 1914 and 1939); people from London, Paris, Berlin, dressed as if for 'La Traviata', are off to the far Caucasus, to drink the *eaux minérales iodo-bromurées* at Piatigorsk, Gelez-nodorsk, Essentouky and Kislodowsk.

Everywhere the new hotels greet them. Some advertise boldly, like the Hotel Gibbon, at Lausanne, where the Master wrote the 'dernier chapitre de son *Histoire de la décadence des Romains.*' (*The Decadence of the Romans* doesn't have anything like the resonant splendour of *Decline and Fall of the Roman Empire*. Even Mr Evelyn Waugh could not, surely, have written a brilliant book called simply *Decadence*.) Others are already acting grand. The Grand Hotel de Lyon says it is 'too important and renowned for anyone to think it necessary to make an eulogy of it with the ordinary resources of *une publicité toujours pompeuse*, an always pompous and often not sincere publicity. It suffices to say that its construction has cost *plus de TROIS MILLIONS*, and that the comfortable and grand luxury are pushed to such a point that it is every day visited as an object of curiosity.'

PILULES DE MORISON issue an *Avis Important* from the *College Britannique de Santé*, Euston Road; French law having been powerless to protect them from imitators, their establishment at 33, rue Louis-le-Grand is FERMÉ, and the veritable pills Morison can now be obtained directly only from the Euston Road establishment. There are a lot of advertisements for waterproofs and funerals (you never knew what you might catch in a foreign country then); and the last advertisement in the book is for mourning clothes, which may be obtained from the *Maison de Deuil Peter Robinson*, 103 et 104, Oxford Street; life and death, for this is not very far from High Holborn and the National Assembly Rooms, *la plus élégante salle de bal du monde*. Perhaps it *was*, in 1863.

The art of the timetable took longer to spread to the East, and, of course, when it did it was subtly modified. If I were compelled to choose only one item from all my timetables I should to begin with concentrate on that for the Ceylon Railways, 1901. Reluctantly scorning the marvellous lists of Special Goods (. . . Tomatoes, Tonic Water in bottles, Toys, Tree Tomatoes, Turnips, Typewriters, Urinals (earthenware). Vegetable Marrows, Velvet Tamarinds . . .) and the note about spotted deer having to be in nets, I should plump for this:—

'*Parties of Choristers or School Children and parties of lads belonging to boys' brigades, under four feet in height, when not less than 20 in number, will be conveyed at half the single fare for the double (return) journey; minimum fare 15 cts. Teachers accompanying the children, choristers, scholars, and brigade lads over four feet in height, and not less than 10 in number, will be charged the full single for the double (return) journey—minimum fare 30 cts.—on production of a letter of authority from the General Manager of the Railway.*'

Ah, innocent parties of brigade lads, bursting out of the train at wayside stops between Colombo and Kandy long ago, some under four feet, others, with voices breaking, over four feet, swarming over the platform, buying mangoes and little cakes from the charwallah, summoned by the shrill whistle of their teacher....

When it comes to modern timetables the wheel is turned full circle. Britain invented the railways, and Cooks invented tourism, and a Cook's timetable is a master-text of the restless modern world from which material could be drawn for a dozen sociological and political theses. Would you know which is the richest country in Europe (or could it be the one that approves most of children)? It is Switzerland, where children travel free up to the age of six and pay half up to 16. In Spain they must pay half between three and seven, after which they count as adults. The Cooks Continental Timetable is the only one I know of that has a Stop Press (it comes out every month, but even so it has these latest bits; *a second-class couchette car of the Yugoslav Railways has been added to the Direct-Orient Express between Trieste and Belgrade—Table 28*). At the top of each page the legend USE COOKS TRAVELLERS CHEQUES is printed upside-down, because that is what the client will read when other agents are looking up a route for him. You can't fault them. *Stalingrad, see Volgograd*, it says in the index.

They know, although they are not telling, why a sleeping-car is represented by a little symbol of a bed, unless it is a *German* sleeping-car, which is shown by a capital S in a square. A restaurant car is a crossed knife and fork, but a German restaurant car is a capital R in a square. They know you can't take more than 200 forints out of Hungary, and whether the Aleppo-Baghdad train runs on Sundays. They know that a timetable is still one of the most exciting books you can read.

HOME AGAIN

❡ England

◆◆◆

WELL, LET'S begin with the only time I ever saw a
kingfisher. I was fourteen, and a boy of fourteen
(or even a man) then wouldn't have known, or cared
to know, that in the Age of Tourism this village, and a
thousand others like it, would later have to be seen
through eyes conditioned by a thousand colour photographs to regard it as Typical. Something wistful about
the actual moment of photographing; hold it—as if
you could hold time, as if your little black box could get
all that moment in. You might get the yellow churchyard wall against which our bicycles lay (end of the
road, a cul-de-sac village), or the squat church over-
looking the river, or the straggly, semi-useful long front
gardens of cottages, with cabbages and hollyhocks. But
you couldn't get the drugged July afternoon silence,
the faint tinny music from a gothic-window-shaped
plywood loudspeaker in a sweetshop, really just a table
with chocolate and lemonade in the dark front parlour
of one of the cottages. And you certainly couldn't get
fourteen-ness, or any other age.

We took the lemonade to the wooden footbridge over
the river (my companion was later to be killed in the
RAF), and there was this kingfisher, a darting tropical
un-English miracle. I've never seen one since, although
I now live practically on top of one of the most painting-

62

famous rivers in the world, Constable's Stour, and look hopefully every time I go down to it.

But the point is that after seeing this kingfisher, and drinking our lemonade, we got on our bikes and went —not to some rural home or holiday beauty-spot lodging, but simply back to the industrial town where we lived—Coventry. The village of Ashow, where the Avon is very young, was a three-mile detour on the way home from school. I used to cycle to Stratford through the Shakespeare Country almost before it was called that. The back way, of course, through the enormous-treed fat meadows of Charlecote, where Shakespeare poached and where one of those inexplicably large churches rears up hugely, as though they had meant to build a medieval* Brasilia, started with this cathedral, and then all gone away, leaving it to three carters and a ploughman.

That kingfisher and that village about four miles from the factory where the Triumph Herald is now made, exemplify something of which our landscape is the supreme triumph—the creation of Inner Space. In more ways than one this is the opposite of Outer Space. It has something to do with England's being physically a small country, a third the size of France; but other small, densely populated countries, such as Holland or Belgium, do not have it, this feeling that a hundred yards down the road, just round that corner, is something utterly different, a region which, nevertheless, when you are in it, will seem absolutely homogeneous, unique, and much larger than it actually is (who would

* actually its nineteenth century (Hampton Lucy).

imagine that in Monsal Dale or at Chatsworth, that stone patrician dream set in blurred romantic hills, you are about fifteen miles from Sheffield?).

I'm not suggesting that France, say, hasn't got a lot of physically different areas. But they're farther apart, bigger, and somehow less contrasty. English Inner Space is a subtle combination of natural differences (the Fens, dominated by Ely as Chartres draws all its surroundings to a point, the Lakes, the Cotswolds, the Dales, enormous empty secret Wiltshire . . .) with a human, individual, loving, one-and-one subdividing.

It is true the French in autumn dress in funny clothes and go after birds and rabbits, but all men of sensibility in their literature do nothing but hanker after Paris. It is impossible to imagine a French Wordsworth. Driving south from Chartres, thinking 'God, yes, Europe, the sacred *paysage* across which swallows from the south have always come to us!' one sees little straight roads leading off to left or right, to hamlets or farms with huge barns on the horizon—and one never feels the slightest urge to go and explore, one knows instinctively they would all look exactly the same. Some Frenchmen are real peasants, but all Englishmen are gardeners, allotment-diggers, makers of quirky villages, constructors of mazes, buriers of surprises among lost woods reached by side roads over hump-backed bridges over which cast-iron notices prohibit you from driving Locomotives or Heavy Motor Cars With More Than Eight Persons.

The only other country in which I have had a trace of this feeling is Germany. Perhaps it is a Saxon or a northern thing. But even in Germany you feel that differences between man and nature, as well as correspondences, are bigger and simpler. You come from mile after mile of haunted forest to an almost defiantly urban little town, with a Kurhaus and an orchestra and extremely complicated cakes. Whereas in the New Forest, nothing like the same size, within an hour you can stand on apparently limitless moors without seeing a house, drive through a paradise of rhododendrons hidden under enormous beeches and firs, pass through a snug village with rather large red Edwardian pubs, emerge on to a little unfenced road (dark woods five hundred yards away across the grass on either side) and see foals, hundreds of foals (this was in June) and horses, and children running, and kites flying, and, if not a kingfisher, I once saw a family sitting on four elegant picnic chairs round a picnic table on to which the wife was just upending a perfect pink blancmange.

Within the hour we were at Christchurch; how could one have not known about Christchurch Priory before, visible from the sea like a vast stranded ship—not known that the place was called Toinham, the Village Between two lots of water, till they found that the unexplained, supernumerary workman who helped the Norman builders by miraculously lengthening a beam cut too short was Christ? There's nothing of that about Bournemouth.

In an enchanting little museum next to the Priory there was an exhibition devoted to the Rev. William Gilpin, Rector of Boldre in the New Forest, a great eighteenth-century expert and theorist about the

Picturesque. 'England,' he said, 'exhibits more variety
... than is anywhere to be seen in so small a compass,'
and also has 'some beauties which are peculiar to itself.'
Among these he puts the mingling of wood and cultiva-
tion and, of course, that supremely English thing, the
hedgerow.

It is impossible to think of 'the English landscape'
without thinking of these three; churches, cottages and
hedges. We have got plenty of real solitudes—especially
if one also counts the purple distances of Scotland and
Wales—but the basic English scene is, of course, this
precisely divided but not formal park, where the
churches and villages grow out of the land because they
are built of local material. There is a 'limestone belt'
of churches running from Gloucestershire to Lincoln-
shire; Suffolk and Norfolk churches are of flint because
there is no stone—sometimes they even have round
towers (no stones for the corner pieces) and thatched
roofs. Many Midland churches are of sandstone.

Nowadays, of course, when anything can be carried
anywhere (and one often gets stuck behind large pieces
of it on lorries) there's a tendency for the hedgerows
to be replaced by wire and concrete, the estate on the
outskirts of the Suffolk or Cotswold village to have green
roofs that look as if they had come from a giant press
in some factory in Leighton Buzzard, and probably
did. One can see how mistaken this is when one looks
at places where people are still compelled to have taste,
as in the Peak National Park, where you may see plenty
of dignified and beautiful council estates made of good

grey stone; the first bright red brick house on the road to Chesterfield hits you like an oath.

But this is where the English genius for symbiosis and assimilation does a tortoise-and-hare thing. Except in the most impersonal and awful of the developments, where they have a communal lawn in front (but who mows it?) and the two parallel horizontal white boards which were the smart thing for fencing a few years ago but now seem on the way out, thank God, there are gardens. One year, building rubble and huge sodden lumps of clay, all round the stark little thing with its green roof; and, almost it seems the next time you pass it, a lawn and a blaze of aubrietia, or rustic arches with hundreds of roses spilling over, or mature-looking gladioli in the autumn. Surely nowhere else is the proportion of neglected gardens so low. For anyone who keeps his eyes open—any passenger, that is—a drive across England is almost like a magnified version of a walk across Hyde Park; you are in a park all the time, but some bits of it are more concentrated than others, that's all.

I read somewhere that the operators of coach tours for foreign visitors have worked out crafty routes that go up and down in the same area, so that they receive the impression of a Vale of Evesham about fifty miles wide. But this is only formalizing what anyone with any sense does when driving about England. As Nancy Mitford has observed, tourists are like ants; and ants can't read maps. The bigger the jams on the main roads, the emptier the secret little valleys and woods over the next fold of land. In the summer season my route to

London is blocked by a notorious four-mile traffic block, often featured in photographs from helicopters after some fine Sunday; and on this Sunday I will have gone to or returned from London through a deserted, private little valley full of waving corn, through spacious and sleepy small towns (in one of which, however, they have a nylon research laboratory) and sometimes visited a little round church, hidden among meadows, which is one of the only two surviving round churches built by the Knights Hospitallers in 1335. I cross defunct railway lines, now simply tracks that march into woods, find a different lane, different manor house, lake, ford, village cricket game, church, wood, arrangement of roofs (how they knew how to put houses on the land, to join one to another, in the old days!)—and always, men in shirtsleeves in the evening sunlight making paths, rockeries, flower-beds, pools, banks, arbours—doing in little what the generations have done at large; that is is to say diversifying, moulding, ornamenting, humanizing, creating Inner Space.

That's not a holiday landscape either; no Beauty Spots (Cars 2s. Coaches 10s.) here, although when one does go to such places, even there one very often only has to walk a hundred yards or so to get a private view. That's everyday England. It's just a matter of keeping one's eyes open. Even for kingfishers.

TRANSPORT SECTION

❡ Cartaker Government

❖❖❖❖❖❖❖❖❖❖❖❖❖❖❖❖❖❖❖❖❖❖❖❖❖❖❖❖❖❖❖❖❖❖❖❖

THERE IS something ambiguous about car park attendants. These humble, anonymous men who materialize out of the rainy cold among the shiny grilles are quintessential pedestrians, descendants of those who used to hold horses' heads for a groat; yet there is also some faint last echo of authority about them, a curious, frail sanctity of power. Above car park attendants come traffic wardens, who are to the real police as prefects are to teachers; then the real police; then the courts and the judges in wigs; then Parliament; then—what? A line of redcoats facing rioters? A voice in a cloud speaking to Moses?

Some quality of the windy, ghostly car park itself enters into the attendant, some tiny, low, civic and human flame. An old, appointed man, a guardian, he broods over a kind of giant adult's nursery, shaking his head over the expensive toys left so higgledy-piggledy— two cars forever sprawled anyhow across the space for three, as though their owners had leapt out and taken to their heels, pursued by police or demons.

Nothing could be deader than a car park, less noticed by the people in it for a few moments, their minds already ahead on appointments, shops, trains. Yet a strange, mute life remains. Many own cars who do not own a house, and when hundreds of them leave their biggest single family possession in this concentrated space one hears faintly the laughter of children on a thousand picnics.

Suppose the balance of life finally tilted towards cars, suppose all the drivers came back at once, smiling, with children and parcels, abandoning such houses as they own? Suppose the rudimentary, gipsy-camp traces of human life—the bits of sacking over winter radiators, the occasional dog on the back seat, the pram on the roof—flowered into a complete settlement, with theatres, restaurants, launderettes, schools, even drive-in churches, surrounding this bleak quadrangle, leaving the wind to hum through empty new towns from Cumbernauld to Crawley, life bursting out where least planned? Then the car park attendant would be king; but now he is an anonymous old man, like a duke in disguise, silently observing us.

Sometimes one feels he is on the point of assuming power. Consider the Royal Festival Hall, where humanity meets symbolically to face the infinite. There, in an ordered social complex, from H.M. the Queen Mother down to the 7s. 6d. seats, among deep carpets, in warmth and blazing light, the people prepare for this majestic organization of sound, this sublime human choice of divine harmony uniting all souls, out of the frightful row the infinite possibilities of sound would make if left to themselves. But this inspiring scene is only possible because 20 minutes earlier most of these people, in hundreds, if not thousands, of cars, were queuing up at a doleful wicket gate on a wet piece of wasteland while one old man fumbled in a sack for change.

Suppose he suddenly said, 'No. It's all off. Nothing tonight. Go home.' What turnings-round, what shouted curses and confusion there would be—even more than there are already.

Car park attendants, vanishing at night, driftingly present by day, look far too vestigial and other to protect one's car. If violent men did force it and roar away in it, one feels they could only lift mild old eyes and hands like a Greek chorus, saying: 'Unruly indeed is the heart of man. He went thataway.' Somehow one does not connect them with the mere operation and mechanism of cars.

So I was glad in a way that it was nearly midnight when I crossed the strange car park, opened the car door, which fortunately I had not locked, and found that the car key was not in any pocket, or amongst the balloons, old apples and shoes under the seat, or anywhere on the ground outside; it was lost.

I had known this would happen sooner or later. Once I was at home in my own garage without the key, which was found six months later inside the piano, by the tuner. The garage man who came then simply clipped a piece of wire on to the positive lead and knew what to touch with the other end, and it started (and he knew the number of my key, too, and got me another before mid-day). If it had been daytime now, with the attendant there, I should have had to ask him if he had a bit of wire. He would have had to hold his end on the positive terminal while I touched experimentally anything looking like a terminal near anything looking like a starter motor; there are so many important-looking cylindrical things down there in the oily gloom.

It would have been like going up to the librarian in some solemn reference library and asking him to explain a difficult passage. . . .

Then I saw a note under the windscreen wiper: *You dropped key. Put on shelf of phone box.* Cancelling my curses I rushed to the phone box and there it was, lovely, lovely key. Surely this was the attendant's work? A bit informal, but then he was not a policeman. Only he would have had the leisured, seeing eyes to notice me drop the key, only he would think of this confident public hiding place, mysteriously sure that, if the wrong man came, lights would flash, alarm bells ring, Z cars converge, shadowy law materialize. At any rate I left him 5s. in an envelope. He seemed worth it anyway, as the custodian of a temple where there had just been a small miracle.

❡ What Do You Mean, a Rag Rf.?

FOR SALE, Fd Cnsl. convtble, Mk. II, 1960. One owner. As new except for 100,000 mls. Still does 80 mph, 25 mpg. What more anyone want? OK, so it blow out bit smoke when start, owner have to keep eye on oil, it still go like bird. Why owner selling then? Ha, clear nasty suspicion from mind, owner wd. cheerfully start on 2nd 100,000 mls., but now got 6 ch., only had 4 when bought btfl. shiny new convtble. It still btfl., shiny, but last h'day, frm. Lahinch (Co. Clare) to East Bergholt (Sfk) in 2 days with w., 6 ch. and luggage convncd owner time come to part with btfl. Fd. convtble, buy prosaic minibus. Fd. just not big enough, that all.

This ad. addr. to convtble-lovers with 4 or less ch. Must still be some. Owner now got minibus, v. nice in prosaic, shut-in kind of way, it got gas ckr., table, about 27 cpbds., drnkng water, blue canopy with poles, seats can make 1 dbl. & 2 sing. beds, & can whizz up mtrwy. at 65 with all these mod. cons., owner not complaining although miss wind in hair; when ch. grow up owner will buy convtble again, if any left, by then; misble. pofaced car-mkrs., agents, grge. men, reflctng alleged pub. taste, will have wished cnvtble—proud, th'bred., individ., charac'f'l obstacle to their doleful, nose-to-grnd. mechan. prft.-making—out of existnce.

While negot. for minibus, owner in many grges, full dreary pea-in-pod slns., always told if he had 1 of them trade-in wd. be eas., trms. arr. no troub. at all. Then

73

man lk. at btfl. shiny convtble, suck in breath, say Ah, wat we call rag roof in trade, no demand for them. 1 man actually say out loud what they all think, he say Of course kids like these things, sometimes we sell one but it got to be gd. cond., not 100,000 mls. like yrs., also yrs. is Pompadour Blue, kids want red. Tip of owner's tng. to say OK, let kids pay damn nearly £1000 (one thou. pd.), as owner did in 1960, if that what they want.

How dare they suck in breath & whistle it out & nod head like that, as tho Fd. frivolous toy? What hell they think owner do with it, gad about with mistress all time? Most of that 100,000 mls. just as bourgeois as mls. on clock of pea-in-pod slns.—taking ch. to sch., w. to shps., owner to stn. But also of course h'day joys unknown to convent'l, po-faced unadvent. parsimon. penny-pinching owners of pea-in-pod slns. now smirkng at convtble-owner, like ants at grsshppr in Aes. Fab. What hell they mean, rag roof? It pfct., weather-prf. hood as gd. as day it bt. in 1960; it been down, ch. laughng & shoutng in back, as Fd. sped up to Ldn., or lifted by cranes on to Fr. docks (& once it flew) & sped thro vineyds., over grt. hills, thro aromatic forests, to Med. That hood been dn. in Italy, when owner richer & had fewer ch. It been up in rain in Ireland, w. & ch. cramped but happy inside. 7 yrs., lustrum of owner's life, grge men are speakng of car owner love. Grge. men obsess. with sordid money vals. wdn't understd., but owner pretty sure Fd love owner too. It never let owner dn. Fan belt brk. twice, but both times right outside grge. where they had spare, put on

74

in ¼ hr., owner sped on with happy, advent., cnvtble life
of wh. po-faced grge. men can know nothing.

If Fd was pea-in-pod sln. & lked. after as lovngly as
this convtble, grge. men wd. thmb thro grbby bklet of
us. car prices & say '£185' (or smthng. misble like tht),
grge men dn't give damn whether it got new tyres,
carpets, batt. (this Fd had five new batt., cd. outlive
five more batts. if fool grge men had wit to see), wd.
still say £185 if gaping rusty hole in floor, seats torn,
tyres bald. Grge men probably think owner's wk. in
mnt'ce of this Fd (of wh. he have no idea—the carpets
lovngly cleaned of old toffees & sick, the Hth. Rbnson
contrptn. for gettng vac. clnr. to reach frm. drawng rm.
window, the wk. with wet-&-dry & touch-up kit) was
simply in deluded hope of keeping resale val. up. Let
owner tell grge men no such thought in owner's hd.,
owner wdn't dream of selling lvly Fd convtble wh. can
still do 80 if there was room for w. & 6 ch. in it. Owner
did mnt'ce because loved it & was proud of it. Owner
also have snkng. suspicion that altho he outside motor
bsnss he have more intuit. sense of qual. in cars than
grge man—he think it feasble to say 1960 was v. gd.
yr. for Fds, just as one say 1959 gd. yr. for claret.

In fact., let owner addr. few general wds. to shrt-
sightd car & grge indust. Quite aprt fr. val. to nation's
health of convtbles (not only obvious phys. advant.,
fresh air, sun—owner has theory you get brown twice
as quickly in convtble, it's comb. of sun & wind that does
it, not that owner self gets full benefit, most of wind is in
back—but gd. for sanity, commun. with trees, sky, can
hear larks, not shut in tight metal box, unreal, schizo,

I WAS JOKING, OF COURSE

accid-prone) let grge men consid. aspect they understd.
best—econ.

Can grge. men not see that as 1 m'fr after another
abands. m'fre of convtbles they will have increasing
scarcity val? There will always be certain no. of people
wantng convtbles, either kids or m. & w. who, like
owner, have kept youth. Moreover, every yr. certain
no. are convt'd to convtbles—1st d. of Spring, cuckoo,
balmy breeze, wind from warm S., they feel blood stir,
urge to escape from dull routine, pea-in-pod sln., say Ha,
let's buy convtble this yr. And each yr. it will be harder
to find convtble, *any* convtble, let alone shiny Pompadour Blue 80 mph 1960 vintage Fd like owner's.

Vintage—can't fool grge men learn frm that wd.?
When owner was boy, father bought bullnose Morris
for £5. Let grge men try to get b-n M. for £500 now.
If grge men had real acumen wd. gladly give owner
his lousy £185, wd. get all convtbles they cd. lay hands
on & wait for boom, wh. owner foresees in less than
5 yrs. Instead of wh. grge men purse lips, say 'Best
you can do with that thing now is run it into grnd.'

Unless this ad. find worthy like-minded purch.,
owner will do no such thing. Even if can't aff. to run
it alongside minibus, will cont. mnt'ce till either, one d.,
enough ch. left nest for Fd to be family car again or
someone so glad to buy convtble with only 100,000
mls. on clock. he give owner more than owner gave for
it in 1960. Seen any time after 6.

¶ Pass along WHOSE Car?

THE MODERNISATION of the railways (in equipment, at any rate) doesn't mean that they are becoming
any less mysterious and shut-in. Rather the contrary:
a steam locomotive is to a diesel as an heraldic king
speaking to his people under a great oak tree is to a
block of government offices. Indeed, now that there
are no longer magic kings, the railway, together with the
post office, is like a kind of vestigial priesthood, dealing
not with the old gods of wheat and grove and roof-tree,
but with equally vital and magic things at the heart of
society—motion and communication, the two essentials
for corporate man.

Postmen, and porters in their new faintly military
uniforms, are subdeacons of a closed, ancient order.
There are hints of a mysterious Book of Rules, codified
long ago from a revelation on some holy mountain, tacitly
admitted to be irrelevant to everyday life except during
fixed lustral, penitential periods called 'Working to
Rule.'

Like old catechisms and formularies with their
stately names for sins, their resounding polysyllabic
lists (such as the Table of Degrees of Consanguinity),
railway documents bring faint memories of barbaric
excesses into a humdrum age. Just as our wild ancestors
had to be restrained from marrying their aunts, so,
once, were they hedged in with stern rules about load-
ing our trains with Carbonized Shoddy Dust, Bengal
Lights, Bran Charcoal, Artists' Sundries (including

Turpentine), Manifold Papers made with oxidizable oils, Oiled Silk (other than stove dried), Oily Bagging, Oily Cap Peaks, Rape Oil Factice (ground) and Zinc Dust or Tutty Powder, to name but a few items on one of the railway forms.

For generations the railways have had this distrustful vision of mankind as a disorganized rabble, clambering on at country stations with their disgusting heaps of oily bagging, scattering carbonized shoddy dust all over the first-class carriages, their coarse womenfolk, in slatternly oiled silk dresses that have never been dried on a decent stove, daubing their faces with tutty powder or worse; and as for rape oil factice....

We are so used to being herded through their little iron wicket-gates under the scrutiny of lantern-jawed inspectors that it has never occurred to *us* to be suspicious about *them*. But now that private revelation, in the shape of the motor-car, has enabled ordinary men to share in the mystery of motion and transport, suddenly we find that this scrutinizing can work both ways; we can do it, too.

It seems appropriate to start with the railways' carparking ticket. Uneasily aware that their passengers now have one disloyal foot in this do-it-yourself world, many stations have acquired dismal pieces of wasteland, as distant as possible, separated from their trains by sidings, often-closed gates, bridges, water-towers (but never a clock in sight) and mysterious huts. On the long, wet, uncovered walks which car-owners must make

78

from these places, men then jump out from one of these huts and demand 1s. 6d.

For this car-owners are given a ticket on which it says, among other things, that the Board, their servants or agents, accept no responsibility in respect of loss or misdelivery of or damage to the motor vehicle, the contents thereof, or accessories thereto, or in respect of any injury to the occupants, by whomsoever caused and whether or not occasioned by the negligence of the Board, their servants or agents.

What do they mean, misdelivery? I'm not asking them to deliver it anywhere, I just want to leave it there till I get back from London (doubtless in a thunderstorm, and rain will cascade on to the driving seat when I open the door). Who are all these servants and agents? I see only this one man in semi-mufti, but perhaps when I have gone he pokes his head inside the hut and says 'All right, lads!' Inside there are scores of these servants and agents, insolent lusty fellows dressed vaguely like Dickensian ostlers. They pour out of the hut. Three or four of them get into my car, and I suppose I am lucky they use it only to race around the dusty cinder perimeter with another Consul, because three more of them have taken a fancy to the 'accessories' in that Bentley over there and are busily prising the clock out of the walnut fascia. But they soon tire of this, and drive it off to misdeliver it somewhere. The Bentley owner has no redress for this, nor for his damaged clock; nor has the owner of that nice little Cortina into whom my 'occupants' have negligently backed my car. Perhaps they feud with a motorized gang from the town, who enter the car park with violent shouting and horn-blowing. But it doesn't matter, they are not going to be responsible for damage by whomsoever caused, never mind the servants and agents.

All right. But I warn them, if anything like this happens I am going to get on a train with carbonized shoddy dust, Bengal lights, bran charcoal. . . .

¶ And East is Anglia

•••

USUALLY IT SEEMS very appropriate that East
Anglia should have been the first completely dieselized
railway region. It never seemed to have much association with steam, the primeval magic of the railway.

Steam was originally blended with northern British
rain-clouds in a grandiose and apocalyptic landscape
with great hills, inclined planes, Vulcan's stithies, sul-
phurous mines, glowering furnaces glimpsed at different
eye-levels—a world in motion and labour.

There was a place for the vertical in all this—Shap
Fell, the iron pillars of high stations, the great arch of
Euston (recently gnawed away by pygmies). But in
flat East Anglia's bright light there are no clouds, no
steam, no furnaces, and all is horizontal. The vertical
serrations in the fretwork of old station roofs seem
aptly replaced by the long squat bands of concrete, the
straight flat cornices, of the modernized ones, which all
looked as though viewed on CinemaScope. Colchester
seemed a suitable place to try out the new B.R. uniform
—grey, dry, matter-of-fact, suggesting Swiss postmen.
Real, British railwaymen have turnip watches, they have
sheds containing enormous waterproofs and stout lan-
terns for going out on wild nights to attend to tall signals
through which rainy winds whistle and moan with a
nordic challenge to action.

And yet, and yet. In its very yellow-brick impersonal-
ity, Liverpool Street, that looks not to any ports serv-

ing vast world-oceans (as do Euston or Waterloo) but merely to the shallow and ambiguous sea that reminds us we might or might not be northern Europeans, does conceal British, mysterious railway secrets. Over one of its doors a sign says GYMNASIUM, with underneath it the name of someone Licensed to sell Spirits and Tobacco. Liverpool Street seems half buried, it is reached down awkward ramps and steps.

Just outside, slyly half-surfacing from this declivity, are more entrances to mysterious railway catacombs than you will see at any more famous and steam-hallowed terminus. In one black curved recess after another, like hellish side-chapels for dwarfs, served by a railed catwalk along which in eight years I have never seen anyone walk, are many little steel doors, which I have never seen unlocked, and hollow caves containing rudimentary pieces of metal, embryo, never-used workbenches, drums of useless chemicals and paint, random selections from the junkyard miles long which the line soon enters. In places the manmade brick has half turned into living rock, streams dribble from it, nourishing strange green stains and flowers.

There are official signs, such as CO_2 DANGER (what do they want CO_2 on a railway for, it's for making soda water?) and unofficial, carefully chalked ones: GAB OF HAINAULT and TILLY THE BUM.

These elvish names explain a lot. I am sure Gab of Hainault and Tilly the Bum don't wear the new uniform. Stooping (for all the bumping and thumping of troglodytic exercises heard late at night from that gymnasium), bright-eyed, they wear little old porters' waistcoats with silver buttons, they carry hammers. Tap tap, it's Gab of Hainault. And Tilly the Bum, heh heh, in rasping goonish voices. . . .

Every now and again (much more again than in the old steam days) a train from Liverpool Street breaks down, always in some desolate near-marsh about seven miles out, dark but for the distant twinkling of name-less misty suburbs. We have gone gloomily along from the start, as if knowing it was hopeless, *duh duh duh DUR,* with every now and then a most tremendous *brrraaahm* from the engine as though the driver were slipping whatever they have instead of a clutch. Then it stops altogether. There is total silence except for one low murmured conversation, a girl's sudden hysterical laugh.

The guard comes through, announcing with disarm-ing cheerfulness that the transfer coil is burnt out or the grobbling nummet has sheared and another engine is coming from Brentwood. The engine we already have shuffles off (oh, it can get along by itself; it just can't pull a train, that's all. What do they expect, if they have a diesel motor driving a dynamo driving an electric motor? It just means there are three times as many grobbling nummets to go wrong. On a steam train the piston turns the actual wheel, and no rot).

After a train-hour (one train-hour equals three ordi-nary hours), spent in composing urgent telephone mes-sages, peering out of the window (where the hell is this, could one clamber across the sodden wasteland, stagger into the nearest lighted home, pant out a request for a taxi?), the engine from Brentwood (Lincoln? Crewe? Zürich?) arrives.

No train has passed us, the line must therefore be clear for a glorious 90 m.p.h. dash to make up. But damme, *this* engine goes *duh duh duh DUR*, just the same. Surely it's not something they've all caught, like that horse flu?

I'm beginning to think it's not the engine at all. It is some sly message passed on by Gab of Hainault and Tilly the Bum, right down the line to Tib of Brentwood, Hop of Witham, Grum of Marks Tey, Lob of Colchester. They were there when British steam came and they'll be here when it comes back.

WORDS, MADAM, WORDS

❧ Scenario for Young Lovers

━━━━━━━━━━━━━━━━━━━━━━━━━━━━━━━━━━━━━━━

Two young lovers are discovered in a rural scene.

He: Yeemy?

She: Yeemy urm! Ahh, so blooful and the bloomy. Doze in the floories, and the greeps all chickering in the weeze. Oh, I'm so hoopy.

He: Urmy leemy! Yoomy a me for ever?

She: Yem, yem. Oh, my neemy barly um, eesh we could settle a hoomy here in the idle bloomy grass! Just a little hoomy own, yoomy for ever. Me in the cooky and dabble the dishpots all sparkle and yum yum the cookery smell, all my dishlove to laybelove. And yoo, come back to the hoomy oom and dingle a dalliance all night long.

He (*Angry, striking one fist against the other*): Ooh, grooh, a gottim a basket of moneybangles to settle a hoomy. Grind it, a basket! Only a lollybag settle a hoomy. Crottit a bangle a bustim workit everyday for pockety; but nagless, hapless, never a packeta boodle to settle a hoomy. Frummit and gudgeon, it's hopeless!

She: Can't a morgidge? A raise a boodle in bankloan?

He: Ha! Yoo seen a bankermen? Frumpy old baldi-gobs, never a smile in banksters for startylife in lovers to settle a hoomy! And the interficious, the goo-between expensymen, agent a tenpercent a stickpalm a grablolly grasping money-baggers. And lawyers a crummyseal. It's hopeless!

She (*stroking his ear*): Oh, loomy leemy barlow, try so do! Gotta wangle a morgidge to settle a hoomy married um, enter a roofy.

(*The scene dissolves to fusty, Dickensian offices. Two old Scrooges at their desks*).

1st. S.: Heretofore a party a blanket aforesaid.

2nd. S.: Wherefore a party a blanket hereafter.

1st S.: Notwithstanding a blanket a party deemed in the blanket.

2nd. S.: Shall assign to the blanket these presents aforesaid.

1st. S.: Until such time or portion thereof as hereinafter.

2nd. S.: Hereinbefore deemed a party of the blanket.

(*Enter the young man He*).

He (*Coughs*): A gentle a gentlemen day.

1st. S.: (*To 2nd. S.*): A possible. Proper a sucker. (*To young man*) Proposition to state it before.

He: I'm in the primy-life, wantim to settle a hoomy and boodle a morgidge.

1st. S.: Yoo gottim a bundle, bully a boodle banklot?

2nd. S.: Morgidge a bundle a boodle youngman. Item a cozener warranty, thirty. Item a registry thirty. Item a cognisance thirty.

1st. S.: Item recognisance party a blanket forty.

2nd. S.: Item a duty thirty. Item commission a stampy hundred and forty. Item in deedibus fusticrustum and searching, seventy-five.

1st. S.: You gottim a bundle eighty percent, fifty percent, deposit a bundle?

He: Only a lone a loan a youngman. Borrow a loan.

1st. S.: Beggar a morgidge no! Speculate in fundibus risky no! Trusty in fundibus here and riskier no! Where a collateral where a security? Creditor morgidge no for youngman. Squeeze in the beltibus morgidge no!

2nd. S.: Paupery youngman no.

He: Crampets and greedybags! Grabbly establishmen! Dead in the top and stonyface rockhearts! I'm a life and primy the future see. Fresh on the threshold and vigoury strong. (*He advances on them. They shrink from him*) And able to labour. Why do you crampet, niminy pinface? Why do you dwindle it, driedheart dustymen? Notary dotards, I'll smote you!

1st. S.: Eek! Police assisteth uth!

2nd. S.: Squeek, he's a freaky assassin!

1st. S.: A bandit abandoned!

2nd. S.: Disordermantisocialist!

1st. S.: So sh'll he murder us eek!

He: Fustibags! Scroogemen! Pinchgrubs! Stinkflints! Hardpates!

1st. S.: Harum scarum!

2nd. S.: Sound the alarum!

(*He backs against the alarm bell and presses it. It rings with a terrible harsh noise. But instead of the police, the girl. She, rushes in. All freeze. She looks inquiringly at the young man, then goes up to him*).

She: Nimmery barlow, nothing at all?

He: Never a boodle; say I'm a beggary pauper.

(*She bursts into wild weeping. The old lawyers try to comfort her*).

1st. S.: Noo, nurdle a weeping.

2nd. S.: Nurmury noo.

87

(They talk over her head to each other).

1st. S.: Childer me own.

2nd. S.: Gone away flown.

1st. S.: All in a weeping.

2nd. S.: No time for keeping.

1st. S.: Tears in a stormy.

2nd. S.: Childer before me.

1st. S.: Moan for the moon.

2nd. S.: Gone away soon.

(They go into a huddle and whisper to each other).

1st. S.: Hrrm. Colleague meself. Careful consider. Applicaforesaid. Condition are willing. Make an exception.

He: Make an exception.

She: Accept us!

1st. S. *(Produces enormous form)*: Certain formalities. Enter a warranty. Bit for the witness.

2nd. S.: Part a blanket as heretofore.

1st. S.: Except insofar as.

2nd. S.: The part of the parcel.

1st. S.: Warrant a treaty.

She: Settle a hoomy, roomy for life!

(She kisses the old men).

1st. S.: Noo!

2nd. S.: Nor!

(She kisses the young man).

She: My loomy leemy barlow.

He: My neemy nurm. Yoomy a me for ever a noo.

(Dissolve to the first rural scene. A very formal quadrille by all four under the trees).

A LITTLE rewriting of history as it would have been, in the language without Latin roots we should have had, if Harold had won at Hastings. With a bow to William Barnes, the Dorset poet-philologist.

GLOSSARY

againclanger: alliterative
againsay: quote, repeat
asf.: (*abbrev*): and so forth
bearsome: patient
clangwriter: (US) phonograph. In England, *writeclang*, gramophone
deathboon: heir
fleefight: coward
folktilth: national culture
freshfind: discover
ingang: invasion
inthought: conscience
lifesome: natural
moreward: positive. Cf. *lessward*, negative
other: (v) to alter
overlead: translate
overthingsome: metaphysical
ringpath: orbit
runningpiece: passage or extract
samenoiselike: onomatopoeic
showbit: example
Southland: Australia
splitbrain: schizophrenic

strongflow: dynamo
switchmeangroup: metaphor
truceful: peaceful
trypiece: essay.—*man*, essayist
twysome: dual
unthingsome: abstract
withalling: consummation
withtaking: concept

I write anent the ninehundredthyearday of the Clash of Hastings; of how in that mighty tussle, which othered our lore for coming hundredyears, indeed for all following aftertide till Domesday, the would-be ingangers from France were smitten hip and thigh; and of how, not least, our tongue remained selfthrough and strong, unbecluttered and unbedizened with outlandish Latinborn words of French outshoot. It is needful only to bethink us how, for showbit, the saying above, 'smitten hip and thigh', might have been written if William the Conquered had been William the Conqueror: 'percussed femur and sacroiliac', or the like! What would then have become of our straight and forthcoming tongue, so fit not only for telling of doing, in tillage, trade or war, but for the unseen inscape of the brain, the bodiless shapes given being by the bard and the thinker?

Our Anglish tongue, grown from many birth-ages of yeomen, working in field or threshing-floor, ringing-loft or shearing house, mead and thicket and ditch, under the thousand hues and scudding clouds of our ever-othering weather, has been enmulched over the hundredyears with many sayings born from everyday life. It has an unbettered muchness of samenoiselike and againclanger wordgroups, such as *wind and water, horse and hound, block and tackle, sweet seventeen, harvest home, blood and thunder, now or never, pie in the sky, hugger mugger, black and blue, bats in the belfry, lock, stock and barrel, a pig in a poke* ...

As that great bookman, thinker, trypieceman and jokesmith G. K. Chesterton wrote anent T. S. Eliot (who upbraided him for too much againclanging), this is the selfstuff of our tongue. 'Must I say,' he wrote, 'I have got a pig in a receptacle? If I wish to speak of one not quite well in his brain must I say he has bats in the campanile?' For so one must do if he lean over backwards to flee from our selfborn againclanging.

The craft and insight of our Anglish tongue for the more cunning switchmeangroups, for unthingsome and overthingsome withtakings, gives a matchless tool to bards, deepthinkers and trypiecemen. Let us, for show-bit, look at one of the bestkenned pieces in our bardic storehouse:

> *To be, or not to be: that is the ask-thing:*
> *Is't higher-thinking in the brain to bear*
> *The slings and arrows of outrageous dooming*
> *Or to take weapons 'gainst a sea of bothers*
> *And by againstwork end them? To die: to sleep:*
> *No more: and, by a sleep to say we end*
> *The heart-ache and the thousand lifesome dints*
> *That flesh is deathboon to: 'tis a withalling*
> *Heartsomely wish'd for. To die: to sleep:*
> *To sleep: mayhap to dream: ay, there's the rub,*

For in that sleep of death what dreams may come
When we have shuffled off this deathsome ring
Must give us halt. There's the highdeem
That makes a woehap of so lasting life:
For who would bear the whips and scorns of tide,
The overgrinder's wrong, the proud man's scorn,
The pangs of backthrown love, the

moot's slow-fare,
The pride of stewardship, and all the spurns.
That bearsome worth of the unworthy takes,
When he himself might his own noise-end make
With a bare bodkin? Who would burdens bear
To grunt and sweat under a heavy life
But that the dread of something after death,
The unfreshfounden land from whose far bourn
No forthfarer comes back, puzzles the will
And makes us rather bear those ills we have
Than fly to others that we ken not of?
Thus inthought does make fleefights of us all,
And thus the hereborn hue of doing-will
Is sicklied o'er with the wan cast of thought
And undertakings of great pith and driving
With this onlook their flowings turn awry
And lose the name of doing.

There has lately been an overleading of the works
of the greater Anglish bards, such as Shakespeare, into
the tongue of the Betweensea Eyots (Guernsey, Jersey,
Sark, asf.). As we have seen these were clutched by
William as a booby-taking after his undergang at Hastings, and ever since have ailed under a split-brain, twy-

some folktilth of lord and villein, conqueror and conquered, upper-kind and lower-kind. It is easy to see
what a falling-off there is when Shakespeare is overled
from his trueborn, lusty Anglish into their bastard and
mingled tongue. In the runningpiece againsaid above,
the strong *lifetime dints* becomes the hueless *natural
shocks. The overgrinder's wrong, the proud man's scorn*
becomes *The oppressor's wrong, the proud man's contumely*, which not only weakens the thought but mars
the five-footer beat (unless the Betweensea Eyotsmen
utter the word *contumely* as *contuMELy*, which seems
unlikely). Most markworthy of all, *Thus inthought does
make fleeflights of us all* becomes *Thus conscience doth
make cowards of us all*. Truly, to overlead bardry from
one tongue to another is a well-nigh undosome thing!

Towards the end of these pieces we shall come back to
the Betweensea Eyots, that awful warning of what
might have happened to our own dear Angland if our
forebears had been overborne nine hundred years ago
at Hastings. But first it is good to look on the moreward
side, to see what happy doom and truceful oncoming
our overgang, the once-and-for-all Saxon overgang, has
brought to the world.

For the truth is that Northern Europe, whence grew
the western folkway which is spread throughout the
nowbetide world, might well have been split and sun-
dered beyond hope, like its southern neighbours, the
small French and Italian kingdoms, if the outcome of
Hastings had been other. Sith Germany, Angland, and
all the United States of Vinland, from Head Horn in
the south to Alaska in the north, speak the same tongue,

I WAS JOKING, OF COURSE

and follow the same folkways, choosing their own free folksmoot, we might be forgiven for thinking of this as foredoomed and lifesome.

Yet it is beyond askthink that in 1066 the world was still in the aftermath and shadow of the mighty Old Roman Overlording; and the strong leaning to look upon the Middlesea folks as the lifesome home and birthspring of all folktilth had already sown in the Germans the seed of a feeling that they were outsiders, cut off from the togetherness of Roman-lorded Europe, going their own way in the deep-wooded, unkenned lands beyond the Rhine.

If Angland had gone the way of the Betweensea Eyots there is every likelihood that our lot would have fallen forever in the Middlesea ringpath, leaving Germany to the full ownsomeness of the outsider, with unforeseeable seeds of strife for aftercoming years.

But this threat was offturned at Hastings. Throughout the Middle Hundredyears Angland and Germany came ever more together, this being needful as an againstweight to the might of France. Angland joined the Hanseatic Brotherhood soon after its beginning, and this was the start of that Anglo-German sea strength which, at the great sea fight off Ostend in 1694, ended Lewis XIV's try at world conquest. After the Truce of Dover in 1695 inside stresses led to the break-up of the French Overlording and the in some ways unhappy 'balkanization' of southern Europe into many little kingdoms, of which Languedoc and All Gaulle, now lorded by Charles the Tall, is a showbit.

It was this same seafaring lore which led to the great

94

Anglo-German outfinding trips over the world, and the freshfinding and settlement of Vinland and Southland. All the wheelthings, maketackles and go-bits which brought the nowbetide world to birth were first up-thought in Angland (the Spinning Jenny of Hargreaves, the steam railway of Stephenson, the strongflow of Faraday, the squirt aircraft of Whittle) and in Germany (the selfwain of Daimler-Benz, the diesel of Diesel) and Vinland (the turnscrew aircraft of the Wright Brothers, the farspeaker of Bell, the quickwriter of Scholes, Glidden and Soule, the clangwriter of Edison).

Everywhere there is freedom of speech, of worship (as thousand-thousands of Aztecs in southern Vinland will witness) and of folksmoot-choosing. There is no upper kind and lower kind, but one happy folk. In the following (and end) piece we shall see, from the showbit of the Betweensea Eyots, how other it might have been for us.

GLOSSARY

breakbit: fraction
breathsound: vowel
craft band: trade union
deedsome: actual
evenstead: balance.—of *Geldgiving*, b. of payments.
feelstring: nerve.—*some*, nervous.
folksway: democracy
folkband: society
folktilth: national culture
forlook: aspect
forthshowsome: significant
fourside: square
geldcraft: economics
geldfind: afford
grail endgame: cup final
headgeld: capital—*some workway*, capitalist system
inscape: imagination
knowcraft: science
makestuff: chemical
outsend: export
outsomeness: extravagance
selfwain: automobile
showbit: example
showcloth: banner
smoothgush: oil
softloud: pianoforte
soothe-woe: consolation

sourcestone: ore

stepfest: a formal dance

tacklework: industry. *T. Quickturn*, Industrial Revolution

talkmoot: parliament—*some workway*, parliamentary system

thousandstep: mile (cf. Lat. *mille passus*).

twysome: dual.—*suchness*, dual nature.

undertown; suburb (an)

undergang: defeat

Vinland: America

warner: monitor

worksmithcraft: technology

Although mighty few folk ever give thought to it (sith the outcome was settled nine hundred years ago) the Saxon Conquest was a near thing; there is hardly any forlook of our folkband, from the Chelsea Bloom Show and the Grail Endgame to the Talkmootsome workway, that would not be altogether othered if William the Conquered had won on the doomy day in 1066.

We have seen in foregoing pieces how our tongue was kept free from outlandish inmingling, of French and Latin-fetched words, which a Norman win would, beyond askthink, have inled into it. We have seen what a strength this has given to our world-kenned storehouse of bardry. We have seen, too, how the off-pushing of French might led to the nowbetide (and farbackstanding) brotherhood of Angland, Germany and the United States of Vinland, sharing the same tongue, the same belief in folksway.

But mayhap even this is not enough to bring home to
the inscape what a Norman Conquest would have meant,
and we are therefore lucky in having a showbit near
to hand in the Betweensea Eyots of Guernsey, Jersey
and Sark.

When these were taken by William, as a boobytaking
or soothwoe win-thing, after this undergang at Hastings,
they underwent the full lustiness of Norman thorough-
ness in overlording (it is forthshowsome that even today Charles the Tall, King of Languedoc and All Gaulle,
has said, in their tongue, that there are but three cul-
tures in the world—*agriculture, horticulture* and *French
culture*). From the beginning the ingangers, with their
feudal 'manors' and strongholds, their lordships of
lands and steadings, and most of all their tongue, rested
asunder from the landborn inlivers; and even after nine
hundred years the two skeins have never become a
onelike yarn.

There were tides when their twysome suchness was
reckoned a strength to them, when Norman warp and
Saxon weft did indeed seem to make a third, freshborn
stuff, a freshborn folk from the mingling of two lusty
bloods. In their farback lore we may read of the Three-
fold Kingdom of the Betweensea Eyots as the main
strength of Europe—nay, of the world. The French
need to overlord, together with the hardihood of the
landborn Saxon foot-warriors, had as end, at one
tide, an overlording of a fourth breakbit of the world,
stretching even to India.

But nowbetide, when the overlording of underfolk is
thought a bad thing, and is not done by any land but

Russia, the sundering between their upper and lower kinds, far from being healed, seems to have come back strengthened a hundredfold. The gap yawns wider than ever, and is the main bottomstalk of their nowbetide woes with the evenstead of geldgiving.

For the truth is that over the hundredyears Norman lord and Saxon villein have merely othered into boss-kind and working-kind. Although the Tacklework Quickturn began in these eyots, and has in other lands led straight to the outcoming of the nowbetide world, there, under the headgeldsome workway, it led to even more gold for the boss-kind and even less for the working-kind, with following kind-strife.

Thus, in this twentieth hundredyear, when geldcraft has out-pushed warcraft as the mainspring of folk-strength, their working-kind still live in the nineteenth hundredyear. When they are asked to make more goods, for outsend, for the good of all the folk together, they will not do so, for they believe it is but for the good of the boss-kind. They are banded together against the boss-kind in Craft Bands, of which the main end is to see that no man does too much work, and to under-take strikes. In our land this word means a lusty blow, as of a man happily working and making—the black-smith *strikes* the iron and the sparks fly, the softloudist *strikes* the keyboard and sweet sounds come forth—but there *strike*, in their tongue, has taken on quite the against meaning, for it means to do nothing, for spite. There are even tides when, the Craft Bands not willing to undertake a strike, the men do it themselves, even to mock moots and mock hanging of them that do not wish to strike, often driving them to feelstringsome breakdowns.

On their side the boss-kind do everything to sharpen this sundering of kinds, from the beginning of their lives. From earliest childhood their offspring are sent to lordsome lerninghouses, where the very cast of their speaking is such as to show this bossness; no longer, it is true, the French tongue, as in the days of their forebears, but a way of speaking breathsounds that straightway shows the speaker's right to wear the Old Lerninghouse Neckband, which opens the door to many reeveships and stewardries in tacklework—even though, by and large, the Old Lerninghouse Neckband crew know nothing about tacklework and worksmithcraft, but have merely a smattering of old tongues—and, as we have seen, the right breathsounds.

It is still quite the greatest boast of such a man that his forebears 'came over with the Conqueror' (William). And another odd thing which has onlived to our own tide, is their belief that the horse is the showthing of overlordship. Many years ago there was a leadingpiece in the *Christian Knowcraft Warner* in which it was said that North Vinland was the most folkswaysome land in the world from having the highest allotting of selfwains. In old folktilths (said the leadingpiece) the overlord-kind took their deedsome names from the horse —the *equitatus* of Rome, the *chevaliers* of France, the *caballeros* of Spain, the *Ritter* or riders of Germany. The horseman high and overbearing on his great beast had the overlordship of leagues of land, unlike the field-working underling, dibbling and scratching the same patch of earth with plough and hoe, lifting his forelock to the feather-hatted, soft-clad, many-hued, awesomely jingling shape of his lord as he clattered by. But with a Tin Lizzie, Jack became as good as his lord, and since more men to a hundred had Tin Lizzies in Vinland than elsewhere. . . .

Without going as far as this it is easy to see that something weird and overawesome still clings to the horse, and the boss-kind are loth to give it up. Their menfolk themselves do not much fare on horseback, except when hunting—a passtime now often thrown into a hodge-podge of bunglement by hair-chinned youngsters waving Against-Blood-Passtimes show-cloths and scattering makestuffs to drown the trackstink. But all boss-kind little girls do so. Moreover, undertown little girls, whose elders wish them to seem of the boss-kind, ride also; their greatest happiness being to have a horselet, horse-legwear, and a little ugly hard hat.

Now, it is true that boss folk do like this anywhere in the world if they can. Even in Vinland, that home of folksway, you may see in their weekly reading-sheets showbits of their boss-kind on horseback, of their young maidens (in such towns as Boston) clad all in white, at old-tide stepfests, for their 'coming-out.' They too have lordsome lerninghouses to which only the children of those with gold can go, and get ready for a birthborn overlordship.

But these are still only here-and-there fun-things, outcrops, not yet bits of their true folktilth (although growing and mayhap soon to become so). Vinland can geldfind such things, sith there are but 180 thousand-

thousand folk in 3 thousand-thousand fourside thousandsteps of land—land uncropped for thousand-thousands of years, stuffed with sourcestone and smoothgush. Even Languedoc and All Gaulle, with 40 thousand-thousand in 212 thousand fourside thousandsteps, with strength to grow their own food, can geldfind a few outsomenesses.

But here in Angland, with over 50 thousand-thousand penned in a scantlack, pinchbeck 97 thousand fourside thousandsteps, we are not in like hap. Everything hangs and hinges on outselling more than we inbuy. But, thanks to the Saxon Conquest, our hearts are high, we are beholden to no one in our brotherhood with Germany and Vinland. The skill and craft, not to speak of brain-cunning and knowcraft, which fathered the railway, the squirt aircraft, the hovercraft and many other freshfindings of the nowbetide world, together with the brotherly striving together for the sake of all folk which is the pride of Saxon men, will see us through to many coming tides of happiness and well-doing.

For if we ever stop to askthink whether this may not be so, we have but to look at the luckless Betweensea Eyots to see what had been our plight if we had not this all-overcoming oneness—if it had been taken from us, nine hundred years ago, by a Norman Conquest.

❡ Escape from Northwin

◆◆◆◆◆◆◆◆◆◆◆◆◆◆◆◆◆◆◆◆◆◆◆◆◆◆◆◆◆◆◆◆◆◆◆

(*After reading several tourist brochures, actual quotations from which are given in italics*).

Ah, wat a hoppy time of expection is to spend in loafing through the pictoreal brochures of hotels and staying-posts of vocations-time, to leaf thruogt the gai and enticing tableaux of holibay retorts wich are traduced into the English tong from such many foriegn lands of sinshine! Truly, atincipacion is none-tenths of harpiness, as one look at the nice colorfult boolets with thier pictures of glumorous sin-baked peaches and antient towns of culture!

Wher sall we goo, with so many nice joly places to temtp us? Shall we og to the Spain, land of blozing sin, of dull-fihgting and fiestas? Here are many typical towns like Elche with its forrest of palmtrees—'*The Sixtime Chapel of the Arboreal Word*' as one of our grear poets has described it. (In England too are grear poets wich celebrate aweful nature, perhap the grearest is Wordsworht; wat *grear* poem is *Simon Lee the Old Hontsman!*) In Spain too are many burstling metropoles as Barcelona, *were many circumciser edificacions group themselves somptuously round the stroller*.

Or we mihgt vacate on a lively Mediterran island as Corsica, where *the networ of Corsica railwags with its comfortable railcars embellish with a perfectly ventilated bar, offers to tourists amazing eassiness and can, if asked, put in circulation special train wihch stop in the muddle of the journey to wonder at the more character-*

istic spaces. Reductions on the price of the simple tickets betrothed. To the mutilate people and war re-formed 50% and 75% Popular tickets ok yearly Warning. The minus you can travel is 80km (return including). Hier pine-barrens and characteristic water-falls are nice for betroothed and honey moan; many return ok yearly wen they are antient-married people!

Or in this day of air-flihgt we can go longer, to Turkey and perhaps at *CELIK-PALAS HOTEL AND HYDRO. For all Health-seekers, Epicureans, Sports-men and Hommes du Monde.* Hier also are the *Hydros of Brussa, excellent for the following diseases. All sorts of Rhumatism. DANTING NUTRITURES (Gout, diabetes, anemia etc). WOMEN'S (ailments, matrix, in-flimation etc); and in old age deprovities (sexual etc). Also historical Roman baths, real jems of existing archaeology with mosaics it is impossible not to wonder magnificence of these incurable chinas!*

In tourist-countrie are abondance of such chinas you can buy from pleasants who make themself, even be-hind Iron Certain such as Titov Veles in Yugoslav (*petrol pomp. Miseum of the macedonian poet, and revolutioner Kocho Racin and a very developed orna-mental crockery; near a lake with an interesting very ancient way of foshing with birds*). Whether you are *homme du monde,* sportsman seeking to fosh with birds or jest a sample tourist, everywhere you will find, as at Paros, fonctionating confortable hotels (and at Paros also *ravishing landscape. Thousands of flies of all colours are covering ground-ivies. At Antiparos the visitor enjoys a merveillous spectacle of unimaginable fantasmagory. From ythe city we go with a little benzine boot, every day).* In Yugoslavia too *the hotels SLAVEN, ESPERANTO and SELCE are constructed directly on the shore and are provided with terrace for baking in the sin and have flying water in all rooms.*

But always for many Englis tourist proposes again the fair Italy. And almost I mad the mind to visit of Santa Marinella, *the gentilly bath-station of the sea-shore of Rome, to bath in the waves wich embracing and sobbing touch the beautiful villas that reflet itself averted in water.* Althought not a *lymphatic person or suffering deficiency calcium, hypertension or athsma,* how I shuold enjoi me the *large bands of pinks of the most sprighly seducing colours, dasies of candid petals that proffer to tourists the welcomely wishes of an em-balming nature of perfumed colours!*

Grearest of all things to attract to Santa Marinella is *the sweetmess of climate. The town enjoys of a soft weather even in winter, sheltered from cold Northwin by the encircling hills.*

Oh peacefully! O bloss and rupture! To escape me from such a drear man as this Northwin! Benson Northwin and his terible wife Glady sNorthwin. Who have not had gentil peace of holibay-sejour destroyd by cold Northwin? Dont you seeing him? You think you are onely Englishperson here, you are losing your hyper-tension and old-age deprovities among the sprighly pinks, and here is coming into the hotel luonge thiss drearful Northwin, who speaks loudy and complaint 'Why is none flying-water in my rooms? Thy have overed my bill too much. Wat danting nutriture, there

is too much oily, I cant ate this foriegn much, brang
me eg and chipps. . . .'

Ho, I get me tiket and go with a little benzine boot,
to Santa Marinella; and dont you dare folow me,
Northwin.

IN THE STYLE OF

❦ All's Ill that Ends Ill

◆◆◆◆◆◆◆◆◆◆◆◆◆◆◆◆◆◆◆◆◆◆◆◆◆◆◆◆◆◆◆◆◆◆◆◆

(For the tenth, or any other anniversary of Suez)
ANTONIO, Duke of Leamington.
ISENIOR, Duke of America.
NIKITA, Prince of Tartary.
DULLEST, Servant to Isenior.
NASSA, King of Egypt.
MOSHEDAYAN, A Jewish General.
HAMMERSCOLD, King of Unopia.
FAGGOT ⎫
BOSHY ⎬ Journalists.
SCOOP ⎭
A Tartar Captain, Diplomats etc.

Act I. Scene I. Before Lancaster House, London.
Bosh: What, thou egg, thou cod's-pudding, thou thin
man, thou piece of nothing, what dost thou here?
Fagg: The same as thou, knot-pate. Faith, we are
gathered here, like pantry-boys of a Wednesday, for
news of the SCUA.
Bosh: I care not for your skua, 'tis, an ill bird, a most
wicked fowl. For doth not your skua advance upon your
goodman gull and seize him the herring e'en out of's
throat?
Fagg: Thou bauble, thou bag of ancient lard, thou'rt
mispris'd from the first, that is, initially, and therefore
I'll instruct thee in these same initials. Learn, then,
that S is for Suez—

Bosh: Marry, a most ungodlike and blaspheming place, for is not Suez your Zeus, that was monarch of the gods, spelt backwards?

Fagg: Peace, fool, else will I make St Ninian's pie o' thy brains. Item, S. Item, C for canal—

Bosh: A vile drain! A most beastly ditch!

Fagg: Peace, I say, pismire. Item, U, which betokeneth users. Item, A—

Bosh: O, most arsy-versy bird. Faith, here's an initial bird will never get off the ground, or perchance fly backwards, sith your A, which is your headman-letter and captains your alphabet, cometh last.

Faggot beats him.

O, O, O!

Fagg: Thou dost well to add thy O to my A, which is for association; for truly this shall be the alpha and omega, the first and last, of thy association with me unless thou now learn the whole, to wit, S, C, U, A; which is, Suez Canal Users Association.

Scoop: A pox o' your bawling, blasphemous, uncharitable throats! Hold your waggish breaths, I say, else will yon whey-faced constable crack all our pates with his truncheon—an ill happening, forsooth, that those who gather news should make it. Look you, here comes the Duke.

Enter Antonio, Dullest, attended by diplomats
of eighteen nations.

Bosh ⎫
Faggot ⎬ : What news, my lord?
Scoop ⎭

Ant: Peace, ho!

(*Aside*, And yet methinks the vile lascivious Moor
Who deems he doth bestride the narrow world
Like a Colossus, 'twixt the tideless Sea
And the multitudinous Incarnadine [or Red],
Is apt for war. But more of that anon).
Learn then, we'll put a girdle round the earth;
With these dear friends, in solemn treaty bound,
Whose argosies with swelling portly sail,
Laden with foison from our several lands
Shall not a ducat pay to Egypt's king.
Exeunt.

Act II. Scene I. A golf course near Illyria, Pa.
Isen: Blow me about in winds! Roast me in sulphur!
Dress me in cheap town-golfer's light attire!
I missed the putt!
Enter Dullest.
Dull: (*Aside.* A foolish, fond old man. Amusing him
with footling golf. Play on!) Dread lord, sole monarch
of the teeming world,
At whose command great bombs have oft bedimm'd
The noontide sun, etc.; by my plan
This other, Eden, demi-paralysed,
Must lose the name of action. Nor is this
All, for if I quench that flaming Minister
Selwyn Lloyd, I know not by what power
They may the fight resume. Know'st thou where
Old Nilus winds him through the spongy meads—
Isen: Is that in Egypt?
Dull: Even so, my lord,
Here doth the wily serpent of old Nile

Purpose a dam athwart the brimming flood;
Too much he hath of water, not enough
Of money—which, if I do now withhold,
Nassa will make a sudden Suez-seizure,
Holding the seas in seisin (that's a joke,
The only one I've ever made). Is't not
Well done?
Isen: Thou dainty spirit, 'tis well done.
Come, let's to golf. Look, out in under par!
It is the course, it is the course! My hole!

Scene II. Another part of Europe. Enter Nikita, disguised as a pacifist. To him, a Tartar captain.
Capt: Dread lord, sole monarch of the teeming world,
At whose command great bombs have oft bedimm'd
The noontide sun, etc., thou who late
Oft smote the sledded Polack on the ice
When Poznan rioted! Th'infection spreads;
Now Stalin's statue, toppled in the dust
Doth make Hungarian holiday.
Nik: I am
In qualities of mercy quite untrained;
It droppeth as the gentle rain from heaven
But not from me. Go, bid the soldiers shoot.

Act III. Scene I. London.
Ant: Fair stands the wind for Egypt (just as well,
Since all my freighted argosies must sail
From Malta as their base). Now England's youth
Is all on fire for this policing act,
Which liberal papers give a grosser name

Though others match their rackets to these balls.
Report my cause aright, and to my soul
Lay flattering unction. Music! Music ho!
Fool (*sings*): Come unto these yellow sands
With France join hands
Cursed it when you have desist
From truce or tryst,
Bomb it neatly here and there
And let Ike the burden bear.
Hark, hark! Bow, WOW!
The watchdogs bark; Wow! WOW!
Hark, hark! I hear
The voice of UNO loud and clear
  Cock-a-muddle-dow!
Ant: I am never merry when I hear sweet music.
Exit, pursued by Russian bear.

Scene II. A desert, near Sinai. Enter Boshy, Faggot and Scoop, disguised as war correspondents.
Fagg: On, on, you noblest English!
Bosh: Aye, wags, fit your hardiments to your stout ceintures! Belay me your culvers, your demi-culvers, your mortar-engines, strew me your candle-mines, prick me on your valiant burgonets and bilbos! O, the brave music of your bombard-rattling thunderstone! Tilly-vally, I am ripe for murther. Thou'rt dying, Egypt, dying! Cry God for England, rhubarb and St George!
Fagg: Faith, what a treasure is here ta'en! By my count 'tis thirty T.34 tanks, a hundred armoured vehicles, a thousand motor vehicles and, look you here (for 'tis a nipping and an eager air o' nights in yon

antres vast and desarts idle), a million blankets from th'
Egyptians won.

Scoop: Sneck up! Thou swag-bellied quatch-buttock
whoreson little tidy-pig! Think'st thou our honour
served by impressing a mountain of gaberdine? In truth
my paper, which speaketh to half the gentlemen in
England now awake, hath not stomach to this fight.

Enter Nassa, pursued by Moshedayan.

Nassa: UNO and Ministers of State defend us!

Exit hastily.

Mosh: 'Twas I that took this booty and these spoils of
war. What, hath a Jew not arms? Hath a Jew not feet?
So all may know, by this feat of arms I may truly say, I
came, I saw, I conquered.

Exit.

Fagg: The sight is dismal
And our affairs from England came too late.

Enter Hammerscold.

Hamm: O proud death!
What feast is toward in thine eternal cell
So many reputations at a shot
Hast thou struck. Go, bid the soldiers cease.

A dead march.

❡ Riders to the Playboy

✦✦✦✦✦✦✦✦✦✦✦✦✦✦✦✦✦✦✦✦✦✦✦✦✦✦✦✦✦✦✦

'MR MURRAY (Chairman of the Electricity Supply Board in Eire) believes that all the peat in Ireland will eventually be used up. The ESB were looking to new sources of power, such as oil. They had considered nuclear power; such stations were, however, not competitive. The Board's engineers had surveyed the tidal currents all round the coast but found no area where this source of power could be used. There was also the windmill experiment at Crooksling, Co. Dublin; unfortunately our winds were too erratic to be used. It might, however, be possible to press into service some of our waterfalls—Torc in Killarney, for example —should the necessity arise.'

Journal of the Institute of Bankers in Ireland.

Cathleen: Let you not be standing by the window, staring at the sea, and it with the waves roaring on it, and the black wind coming off it, under the window-sill, the way you'd catch your death, and you an old woman.
Morosia: And what way would I be getting warmer if I came to the fire? Sure 'tis only one bar in the element, and it not red enough to stop a mouse from shivering.
Cathleen: 'Twill be better when the Electricity Board has harnessed the tides and the power of them leppin' like a thousand horses out in the bay.
Norah: Whisht, Cathleen, is this a time to talk of the Board, and herself standing lonesome at the window, and the heart of her sorrowing for a sight of the ship

and the fine men on it that is going to harness the tides, and it going to the north round the green cape, and her son Michael with them?

Cathleen: 'Tis nine days since they went round the green cape, and they laughing on the decks, and the great devices on them for measuring the tides, and their little electric screwdrivers that be insulated to the world's end.

Morosia (*keening*): Ah, Michael, and him with a screwdriver bright as a sword to bring the electricity out of the roaring sea to help Ireland; and now he's drowned on me! The men came up the path from the sea to this house, carrying a little bit of a rusted screwdriver. 'Twas all they found. 'Tis the black curse of an old lonesome woman I do be calling on their electricity.

Cathleen: 'Tis no use for to stand there keening since Tuesday was a week. 'Tis little you'll see of Michael again, and 'tis little current he'll know from this day out but the current of the roaring sea.

Norah: Whisht, Cathleen! To talk so to your own mother, that is after losing her son!

Cathleen (*passionately*): And I after losing my brother —and a better man he was than my husband that lies in his shroud there (*pointing to inner room containing the man falsely supposed to be dead that you always have in Synge*).

Norah: Shame on you to speak of a man that did no harm, and him a turf-cutter, even though the drink was on him.

Cathleen: Aye, a turf-cutter, like his father and his father's father before him. And where would the likes of him give us enough power even to light a 30-watt bulbeen? 'Tis glad I am this day to be free of him, for I'll marry Donagh that is to make the electricity from the little dancin' atoms. O, I'll leave the lonely glen where there do be nothing but the little weak bulbeens that do be flickering with the sickly current that's in them. I'll travel the royal vale of Munster and the great lakes of the Shannon, by the factories with the little Japanese men working in them; and I'll travel so by the side of a man that is to bring 220,000 golden volts from Ardnacrusha to the town of Dublin. Let my mother not be laying the long curse of hell on the sainted electricity that is to make Ireland a great land o' the world, with the people leppin' in their houses to the sound of their radios, and the bones of them warm by their electric fires, and all the air full of a great humming of volts and ampères, the way a lonesome bird coming out of the western sea would be dazzled by the shining of a great light, all over Ireland!

(*Enter Donagh, a nuclear power station engineer*).

Donagh: Cathleen! 'Twould take all the sodium lighting in the wide world to match the light in your eyes!

(*The presumed corpse on the bed within rises. It is Cathleen's husband, Dan*).

Dan: Ah, 'tis run away to the divil and the dynamos would you, with the little sparkeen here, and the head of him full of wheels like a little meter going round!

Cathleen: Glory be to God, I thought you was dead.

Dan: 'Twas nothing, only a gallon of poteen. For 'tis not only your electricity can warm a man or lay him out like a holy statue of God. (*To Donagh*) What, is it still here you are? Let you be going out of my house, or I'll give you a clout on the skull will show you bigger sparks than ould Michael Faraday ever caught in a jam-jar, bad cess to him!

(*Exit Donagh hastily*).

Cathleen (*staring sadly out of window*): Ah, Norah, 'tis yourself will be the only one of us to marry an electric man. I see the little fellow from Crooksling coming up the hill, that has the queer windmill for turning his dynamo.

Norah: Is it Christy, then?

Cathleen: It is so.

Dan (*roughly, to Cathleen*): Let you come with me, then; for I'll not be speaking to any more of them little jumping sparkeens; though the devil knows I've a mind to break the bloody circuit on him.

(*Exit with Cathleen. Enter Christy*).

Christy: Norah, is it yourself? And is it decided you have? Ah, let you come with me. 'Tis a grand place for a girl with the fine volts in the eyes of her, is Christy's electric windmill; for what would you hear only the sweepin' of the great sails, and the wind from the west rushin' through them, and the dynamo hummin' like a royal cat in the court of Queen Maeve herself.

Norah: 'Tis the poet you are, Christy Colum, and not an electric man at all.

(*Enter Sean, Norah's fiancé, a conventional power station engineer*).

Sean: Did you not promise before Father O'Brien to marry me? And amn't I the only true electric man in the place, and me after studying in the foreign lands

116

where the oil comes out of the ground like the water of Moses? What would you do with the likes of him in a windmill? Will he light the town of Dublin with his windmill? Is it work for the Board he will? Is it a pension he'll be enjoying when the both of you is old and the current of life running low.

Christy: Pensions! 'Tis the talk of an old man surely. 'Twill be the sad day for Ireland, and the birds hovering over the lonely hills and they with the great pylons marching over them, when 'tis took over by the likes of him and his Board and his oil and his pensions! Is it marry him you would and live by a great ugly power-house, and the lines from it all over Ireland like a spider-web, and the wild spirit of the electricity caught like a poor beast in a cage? Or is it with me, and the electricity a wild joyful surprise, coming like the gift of heaven only when the free wind of life blows over Ireland? Or maybe I'll be coaxing it out of the great waterfall of Killarney.

Sean (scornfully): 'Tis nothing but tinker's electricity you'll have.

Christy: 'Tis the true electricity of the world I'm after making, for 'tis nothing but me own name in the tongue of France. Did you never hear of the coulomb, that is the amount of electricity moved by one ampère in one second? Christy Colum, that's the very same as Christy Coulomb.

Norah (softly): Your ways are my ways, Christy Coulomb, and the ways of Ireland. Let us be going now. (Exit with Christy. The others stare after them for a moment, then all start keening).

❡ Suffolk

Now to the counties written up in *Punch*
Is added Suffolk. Coming to the crunch
I see no method fitter than a slab
Of rhyming couplets in the style of Crabbe
(Or sometimes triplets; take it not amiss   ⎫
If I, like Crabbe, the Muse's extra kiss   ⎬
Denote by brackets at the side, like this).   ⎭
To come as near to Crabbe I dare not hope
As Crabbe himself came anywhere near Pope;
This is a verse in which will not be found
Wild flights of fancy far above the ground.
At best, it gives the essence of the place,
But at the worst, e'en Crabbe is commonplace.
Where would you find a poet of today
Who'd write of Aldeburgh in the following way:
Where hang at open doors the net and cork
While squalid sea-dames mend the meshy work?
Though, on the other hand, one must admit
In scenic lines he made a job of it,
Thus: *when the cattle as they grazing stand*
Seem nobler objects than when viewed from land.
(How true! What memorable lines to quote
When one is viewing cattle from a boat!)
Needless to say, in these our affluent times   ⎫
The lifelike gloom, the poverty and crimes   ⎬
That Crabbe evoked in tales like *Peter Grimes* ⎭
Seem very far removed from Suffolk now
That no more Suffolk Punches speed the plough,

But massy Harris-Fergusons and such.
Nor would the wealthy farmers relish much
His view of Suffolk as poor farming land
With not much topsoil and a lot of sand:
Lo, where the heath, with withering brake
                                    grown o'er,
Lends the light turf that warms the
                            neighbouring poor;
From thence a length of burning sand appears,
Where the thin harvest waves its wither'd ears;
Rank weeds, that every art and care defy,
Reign o'er the land, and rob the blighted rye.
With hormone mixtures they have changed all that;
Sleek are their Jaguars, and their bank-books fat.
Wire fence, not hedgerow, marks the prairie fields
Where concrete barns hold scientific yields
And long low buildings, unadorned and stark
House broiler chickens, mostly in the dark.
The turfy heath near Aldeburgh affords
Nor is East Bergholt now the only place
The gull that o'er the clubhouse soars and whirls
Sees down the coast expensive schools for girls
And cots to which no weary peasants wend—
Stockbrokers live there every fine week-end;
And farther north still choicer sites they pick
At Southwold, still unspoiled, or Walberswick,
Where well-known men our bustling scene avoid;
Thus Anthony Sampson, and thus Clement Freud:
Then there's another smartish yachting place
At Woodbridge (near the US Air Force base).

Who (for a quiz) were called The
                                  Woodbridge Wits?
Why, Barton, Churchyard, George Crabbe Jun.,
                                   and 'Fitz',
Gruff old Fitzgerald, of Rubaiyát fame
Who, reared in Suffolk, back to Suffolk came
(His quatrains have a third, unrhyming line
Like that; first, second, fourth are all the same).
Thus may be seen from what rich soil there springs
The Festival of Britten summer brings
Each year to Aldeburgh, when the little town
Is filled with artists of supreme renown.
The finest music (in the church) is free,
No need to post in March the booking fee
To hear the Purcell Singers give delight
With Imo* in the middle of the night.
Ah, what a wealth of choice the programmes show!
When two things coincide, it's hard to know
Whether to stay for Bream or (jolly jape!)
Hear handbells in some wooden hut near Snape;
And if at last the music starts to pall
There's E. M. Forster in the Baptist Hall.
Here in the words of Crabbe you have it all:
The Tavern's pleasure or the concert's charm
Unnumber'd moments of their sting disarm;
Playbills and open doors a crowd invite
To pass off one dread portion of the night;
And song and show and luxury combined
Lift off from man this burthen of mankind.
Not only concerts, but the times between

* Imogen Holst.

Amuse the student of the social scene.
In Festival Club, in hotel lounge or bar
How much prestige it brings to know a star!
Friend talks to friend, but looks not in his eyes,
Scanning the room for gods to recognize
Or to be smiled at by (Ah, fate unkind!
Peter was smiling at someone else behind;
Undaunted still, the friend soon tries again,
Who last year really got a nod from Ben).

Letter II

Cities and towns, the various haunts of men
Require the pencil; they defy the pen
Said Crabbe—though surely one could find
                                    a ground
For turning this surprising statement round?
Writers are urban, painters love the sky,
Else will their art, too much abstracted, die.
Suffolk may claim the first one to have seen
That trees should not be painted brown, but green;
His father's windmill taught him as a boy
Which clouds mean trouble, which mean
                                    summer joy.
Sketching the aery regions with delight
Constable did not claim, though well he might,
To be the first Impressionist. That chance
Was grabbed by those who copied him in France.
Long was his lovely county hid secure
Since no commuter lived who could endure

The railway service dim and incomplete
That vaguely led to dingy Liverpool Street.
Now all is changed. The speedy diesels roar,
One every hour, far quicker than before,
And soon all dual-carriageway will be
The road from Woodbridge up to EC3.
Now is this land of open field and heath,
Of sweeping skies with peaceful towns beneath,
Farmsteads and cottages washed in pink or white,)
And fine flint churches rising on the sight,
Doomed by the planners to an urban blight,)
Constable's home will have two thousand more
In green-roofed shacks by 1984.
Nor is East Bergholt now the only place
Where the bold speculator shows his face;
Nowhere in Suffolk is, but such schemes can
Borrow the dignity and style of plan
And the bold speculator may deride
Any that dare to swim against his tide;
'The people must have homes'; with words
                                    like these
Suggesting crowds of homeless refugees
He shames all opposition. Yet a doubt
Remains, though none will dare to speak it out,
That really homeless people won't come here—
£4,000 would be a bit too dear.
Who shall withstand him, when the plans are made
By councils full of tradesmen, seeking trade?
Who is there cares, when landscapes gently grown
Through every generation but our own
Die in a month, a thousand years of love

Bulldozer-crushed in one almighty shove?
Will not the farmers stay the raiding band?
Not on your life. They queue to flog the land.

Letter III

Say, is there naught of comfort to be had?
Must all decay? Must every change be bad?
Let not the picture be so full of gloom,
Not every Suffolk poet should assume
With Crabbe, *a Muse like mine, to satire prone*
Would fail in themes where there is praise alone
(Though Letter II would have been much

                            more dour

If written by our Poet of the Poor).
What though the football fame of Ipswich Town,
So quickly risen, fall more quickly down?
See, where the Civic College maids and youths
In a fine building learn eternal truths!
What though from Sizewell, with atomic power
Enormous pylons the fair plain deflower?
Still you may find, a mile away from these,
Magical villages hidden under trees,
With fine straight people, who say *that* for *it*;
'That's time,' they say, 'owld Suffold changed a bit.'
(*Pace* De Gaulle, they've never quite lost touch
With Europe, least of all the neighbouring Dutch).
Though new life stirs the county's ancient soil
Let one line stay, of all the poet's toil:
Suffolk is far too good a place to spoil.

123

ℭ The Seduction of Figaro

✦✦✦✦✦✦✦✦✦✦✦✦✦✦✦✦✦✦✦✦✦✦✦✦✦✦✦✦✦✦✦✦✦✦✦✦✦✦✦

> Philip and Stella, well off but bored with each
> other, invite two happily married friends—Jane
> and Martin—to spend a weekend with them.
> Stella suggests to her husband that they play a
> game. If he can seduce Jane she will get him a
> Dalmatian. If she seduces Martin he buys her a
> Monteverdi record . . . the first of a group of
> operas which are being commissioned and which
> will deal with happenings—bizarre or ordinary,
> comical or tragical—that belong very decidedly to
> the everyday world.
>   —Radio Times on "The Arrangement."

I WAS MOST unfortunately prevented from seeing
this opera by one of those situations that belong de-
cidedly to the every-day world. As a matter of fact our
weekend visitor, Harold (tenor), was stabbed by his
mistress Martha (contralto). Their visit began smoothly
enough; they told us some amusing stories about their
recent cruise on a Dutch boat whose captain was prevented from retiring by some legal hold-up. But on the
Sunday Harold went out shooting, with silver bullets,
in a local wood just off the A12, and while reloading
he was attacked by a very large, red and green serpent,
from which he was rescued by three ladies to whom it
apparently belonged.

They took him to what appeared to be a disused
cinema, where a lot of rather awful old men in night-
shirts urged him to marry a girl (soprano) called Pamina
or it may have been Margaret; at any rate, Martha came

upon them while this girl was going on rather hysterically about some jewels; Martha suspected they were a gift from Harold, although the girl kept saying they were from the Devil. After stabbing Harold, Martha, mad with grief and remorse, made a last passionate farewell in some strong moonlight which had appeared rather suddenly, afterwards taking poison and jumping from our battlements, narrowly missing the garage roof. We were still trying to sort out things with the police, soldiers, brigands, peasants, gipsies and waiting-women when *The Arrangement* came on. Also, of course, we can't get BBC-2 in our part of the world.

The curious thing is that in the mad old days I once wrote an opera libretto myself on exactly the same theme (unhappily I later had to burn it, one bitterly cold night when we had a little sempstress in for drinks). A few of us had been talking about the absurdity of opera plots; surely it was a flight from reality to use mythological or historical themes when all the richness of music was waiting to help the ordinary opera-goer by heightening and illustrating situations familiar in his own life.

'For instance,' I said, 'take the everyday situation when a couple play the game of seducing their weekend guests. A humdrum subject, you may feel; every married couple knows that flat feeling on a Friday when people are coming down for a seduction, the boredom with the endless trivial round that sometimes goads the weaker into anti-social fidelity. Yet Coward made it sparkle in *Private Lives*; why shouldn't opera meet the challenge too?'

'I can give you a plot from real life, old boy,' drawled Guido, a rather well-off friend of ours (the only one not a writer, painter or sculptor, he was something in fabric research and testing), married, for some reason, to his wife, Amanda. 'Mandy and I had this couple down a fortnight ago, can't remember their names. . . .'

'Marvin and Stella,' said Amanda.

'No, that was last week, the Gabrieli and the boxer. Well, anyway, I promised her a Monteverdi. . . .'

'I've got the lot now except a couple of motets for three voices, *Lapidabant Stephanum* and *Lauda Sion*.'

'And would you believe it, this girl—Yvonne, yes, that was it. I remember she had a gold tooth. Must have been French. Well, she said I could seduce her if I gave her a Monteverdi record. So on the Saturday morning I popped into The Music Box, and there was her husband. . . .'

'Jimpson. That was his Christian name. Jimpson and Yvonne Something.'

'Yes, and this Jimpson was coming out with *Il Combattimento di Tancredi e Clorinda* for what's-her-name, Yvonne, and *Il Ballo dell'Ingrate* for greedyboots here, who'd made the same proposition to him.'

'Greedyboots yourself. You asked that girl as well as me for a Dalmatian.'

'Yes, true. Can't think why, I hate them, they always make me think of measles. Maybe it was association; Dalmatia is next to Monteverdi.'

'No, that's Montenegro.'

'Well, there aren't any dogs called Herzegovinians.'

'I don't see what that proves. There isn't a composer called Bosnio.'

'Never mind. Anyway, this Jimpson and I had a bit of a natter about women and we were just turning into the pub with these four records for a quick pre-lunch when we met the girls coming down the street with four Dalmatians. In the end we took all the records back to the shop and all the dogs back to the kennel. We had quite an amusing weekend, with each other. And, of course, it was miles cheaper. . . .'

A pity I burnt the libretto.

EVER LET THE FANCY
❡ Hair, Hell and Heaven

++

THERE WAS A story in the *Sun* recently about parties
given 'at the Kensington flat of a wealthy businessman,
where teenagers were given LSD, the powerful drug
that gives visions of heaven and hell ... nearly all the
teenagers ... *from middle-class families, mostly students,
hairdressers*' (my italics) '*and people on the fringe of
show business* ... teenagers in Chelsea are said to be
chewing blotting-paper impregnated with the drug.
Others inject it or swallow it with lumps of sugar.'

*Scene: Harris's Hairdressing Saloon. The 1st. Hair-
dresser, smiling madly, is sweeping up hair cuttings
from the floor. The 2nd. H. sits in a corner, staring
with dread at a hair-dryer.*

1st. H.: Brown grass, it's like sweeping a lawn of
brown grass. Brown grass, across the mouth blown.
Brown grass, mown grass, white grass, green grass.
God, I feel witty. The earth's old white hairs are witty
and wise. Must write that down. Green hair, brown
hair. Brown grow the brasses, O. And every hair a
liddle iddle diddle follicule, maginified a million times.
Liddle iddle tubes, maginified, look! I know everything
(*Enter a regular customer, Mr Hardcastle, 53, a dealer
in plumbers' sundries*). I know who you are, liddle iddle
green-haired man. You are Mr Balson Bolson Everett
Crumpson, a fetch-gather and grassman, of Yebberley

Buildings. Yebberley, ah ha ha ha (*shrieks with laughter, collapses into chair*).

Mr Hardcastle (*impassively*): Short back and sides. Where's Mr Harris then?

1st. H.: Mr Harris, went to Paris, in a bowl of water: to drench a wench in French; the naughty daughter. (*Stares at top of Mr Hardcastle's head*). O shorter back an' sides, your head seemeth an' beameth. On thy bald awful head, O sovran blanket! I feel free, free, floating over your shining head. An atomy molecule follicule over your liddle iddle head. Free as a tweezer (*sits down in other chair, repeats this solemnly*). Free as a tweezer. (*Enter Mr Harris*).

Mr Hardcastle: What's this then?

Mr Harris: I'm sorry, Mr Hardcastle. I've just been to the bank. Just taking the old L.S.D. (*mirthless laugh*). So have they, by the looks of things.

Mr Hardcastle: Who are they then?

Mr Harris: My assistants. They're from middle-class families.

Mr Hardcastle: What have they been doing then?

Mr Harris: Taking this drug, LSD it's called. It gives them visions of heaven. (*Absentmindedly switches on hairdryer*).

2nd. H. (*screaming*): Yarggh! Staring at me! It's alive! Blowing foetid breath at me! Burning me! The eyeless snake of hell!

Mr Harris: Or sometimes of hell. They don't seem to be able to tell in advance.

Mr Hardcastle: What do they take it for, then?

1st H.: Why did you say 'then', then, then? Liddle

bald-haired man back and sides, you are part of Everything-Karma too. Let me float, singing like a god, over your liddle domed infinite head, back an' side, to an' fro, up an' down, pro an' con, time an' tide, Bill an' Ben ... (*seizes scissors*).

Mr Hardcastle: No you don't then. Cut me ear off. I'm going somewhere else then.

Mr Harris (*hastily*): No, I'm terribly sorry, Mr Hardcastle, please let me do it. I'd no idea they were like this. They came to me after being Fairy Soap Men.

2nd. H.: All we could get after R.A.D.A. Fringe of show-biz. We were at Repton and R.A.D.A. together (*Shakes head vigorously*). Thank God it's worn off. It was hell that time. I do apologize, Mr Harris, and, er, to you, sir, Mr Hardcastle.

2nd. H. (*whispering fiercely to him*): Shut up, Barry, you fool. Do you want to go back to Fairy Soap? Remember our plan for our own salon. Remember Vidal. (*Leads 1st. Hairdresser, who is still smiling beatifically, into small side room, after which he returns*). I say, I do apologize most frightfully. Would the gentleman care for a vibro-massage?

Harris: It's all right, I'm doing him. Very well. But next time, out you go. You can make the tea now (*exit 2nd. Hairdresser*). They're all right when they're off the stuff. Middle-class boys do give the place tone, you know. (*Re-enter 2nd. Hairdresser with tea. He offers it to Mr Hardcastle*).

2nd. H.: Would you care for a cup of tea, sir? Compliments of the management.

Mr Harris: See what I mean? He does it beautifully.

Mr Hardcastle: Where's the sugar then? (*Mr Harris takes from the shelf a saucer containing two lumps of sugar and, not seeing the dismay on the 2nd. H.'s face, offers it to him*). Excuse fingers. (*Mr Hardcastle puts it in his tea and drinks. Enter 1st. H., looking like hell*).

1st. H.: Paradise lost. I'm falling, falling into hell. I must go for another 'trip' (*stares wildly at empty saucer*). Where's it gone? It was there! I put it there!

Mr Hardcastle: Yarrgh! Arrgh! You've cut me ear off then. The snake's coming at me then! Biting me ear off. . . .

⦑ Wash Me in Steep-down Gulfs of Liquid Mr Sands!

It's AWFULLY difficult to imagine the Royal Festival Hall on fire. All that concrete—and where there is wood it is in great open shiny expanses, you feel it couldn't blaze up all at once, the fire would have to start in some actual corner of the shiny expanse, and everybody would see it. Everything is so modern and clean, there aren't a lot of fussy little green rooms with muslim curtains and ribbons and bibbons and wicker chairs and Indian screens and cupboards full of bustles and bobbles and other combustible clutter. And always there is this sense of massive concrete behind and underneath such wood as there is, a built-in firebreak.

Yet the Crystal Palace, they have obviously said to themselves at the Festival Hall, was made of glass, and that burnt down. It couldn't happen here, but we'd better have a drill all the same. Some GLC genius, therefore, has caused to be printed, framed, and posted on the walls of every room and corridor of the non-public part a set of fire instructions which must be the most dreamlike and unreal anywhere in the world.

In the event of a fire occurring in any part of the building the word FIRE must on no account be used within the hearing of the public. The code word used on all occasions is 'MR. SANDS'; therefore, 'Mr Sands is in the Grand Tier' would indicate that a fire had occurred in that position.

All personnel on receiving code message must pro-

ceed to their respective positions as allocated by the Chief Steward and Staff Supervisor as quietly as possible and stand by doing nothing to attract attention. . . .

When the fire is extinguished the message 'Mr Sands is all over' should be circulated to all personnel. . . .

Now it is, just possibly, not a lunatic idea to have some code word instead of *fire*. Some neutral word, like *blue*, or *meeting*, or *interest*, or *biscuit*, would do nicely. Urgent messages, hissed from the sides of their mouths by the personnel, such as 'there is a biscuit in the Grand Tier' or 'the interest is all over' might mystify the audience, but it is just possible to imagine them. 'Mr Sands' is different altogether. Once this name, divinely inspired, flashed from who knows where into the brain of the writer of these instructions, his task changed from boring bureaucratic routine to creation, fantasy, indeed poetry. The unreality of his task, the difficulty of envisaging a fire among all that concrete, led the writer into the dreamy, passive state of the poet when he is heavy with a poem. The mysterious spark flashed, and Mr Sands was, literally, fire-born.

It is wrong to think of Mr Sands purely as an anticlimax, a piece of sublime bathos; although it is true this is the first and most obvious impression, one does feel that if they can connect such a prosaic-sounding name with the majestic and raging element of fire they could do it with the high art of music as well. One tries to imagine what kind of music De Falla's *Ritual Mr Sands Dance* would be. Or what Wagner would have done if it had been necessary to find a 'Magic Mr Sands motif' (for the bit in the Valkyrie where Brunnhilde lies sleeping in a whole circle of Mr Sands)? One likes to think of the public address clicking on just before a concert, and the announcement 'Ladies and gentlemen, there has been a slight change in the programme. Instead of *The Mr Sands Bird Suite* by Stravinsky the orchestra will play *Music for the Royal Mr Sands Works,* by Handel.' Or of the choir, at a concert with a patriotic tinge, singing

> *Bring me my bow of burning gold!*
> *Bring me my arrows and my brands*
> *Bring me my spear! O clouds, unfold!*
> *Bring me my chariot of Mr Sands!*

—and come to think of it, there is a famous madrigal which becomes changed for ever once one has read this notice

> *Mr Sands! Mr Sands! My heart!*
>   *My heart! (fa la la, etc.)*
> *O help, alas, O help! Ay me!*
> *I sit and cry me*
> *For help, alas, but none comes nigh*
>   *me (fa la la)*
> *Mr Sands! etc.*

And come to think of it even more, have they seriously considered the possibility that under the present rules one of the personnel might find himself in the position of having to shout out 'Mr Sands is in the Ladies'?

Of course they haven't. You can bet your boots that if there was a fire they would say *fire,* just like anybody else, and would doubtless be efficient and well-trained about not shouting and about knowing where all the equipment was—Mr Sands extinguishers, Mr Sands hoses and even Mr Sands sand buckets. My theory is that these instructions are really the codification of a private game played by the personnel to relieve the tedium of standing around while all that endless music is going on, day after day, night after night.

Anyone who has ever asked an attendant at the Festival Hall anything, or tried to get a drink after a concert (or during the interval for that matter) will have noticed that they all seem withdrawn, thinking about something else. Well, what they are thinking about is this game, *Mr Sands*. It is a combination of a sort of patience, Zen exercise, and guessing-game.

You have noticed that Festival Hall tickets are marked Red Side and Green Side, and that the uniforms of attendants are also distinguished accordingly? These are, in fact, the opposing sides in the game of 'Mr Sands', another round of which begins when the audience are safely ensconced in their seats and that noise has begun again which they have, incomprehensibly, come pouring in to hear (cluttering up nearby pieces of rough waste land with their cars, so that it is necessary to have one man fumbling in an old sack for change to stop them all getting in free, or quickly or conveniently).

Each side chooses its Mr Sands, and the object of the game is, of course, for the opposite side to catch him. But it is a great deal more sophisticated than mere hide-and-seek as there is a strong element of bluff.

Messages mysteriously relayed over house telephones or carried up in the orchestra lift or some other backstairs grapevine, that Mr Sands is in the VIP suite or a double-bass case, may result in loss of points if the player finds in the VIP suite a real VIP, or in the double-bass case the Mr Sands of his own side. Indeed the highest penalization is for letting the game impinge on the public at all, beyond a sound of suppressed giggling heard round an angle in a corridor, an abstracted look in the eyes of a bar attendant 'doing nothing to attract attention,' oblivious of the fact that this is half-time, the public are milling all over the place. The gong that calls us back to the concert is to the personnel the whistle for the second half of 'Mr Sands'.

The two central figures of the game are, ideally, two identical men in short white tunics, rather like Mr Therm, with those trade-union-leader glasses that have a thick black rim at the top and no rim underneath. They are very light of foot, with a magical skill at popping up in unexpected places; swift and insubstantial as rumour; partly like disembodied Arthur Askeys and partly like—well, like something you don't at all expect in the Festival Hall—like little tongues of fire.

◖ The Great Umbrella Serial

FOR THE READER there are four kinds of book; those one has read; those one hopes to read when one is this old man in a smoking-jacket in some marvellous firelit library (all those chaps one is vaguely aware of—Boethius, Robert Musil, that great Italian pessimist, Leopardi, Leonardi. And wasn't there another rather grand one, Vico?); books one wouldn't read if they were pushed under the cell door after 20 years' solitary confinement—*The Carpetbaggers*, anything about lesbians or homosexuals, especially French ones, any book in which inarticulate people from some bogus sociological group speak to a tape recorder, any James Bon. . . .

Goodness, must reluctantly stop to leave room for the rest of this piece, which concerns a supreme example of the fourth kind—books which actually to read would be an anti-climax, books whose mere titles must be allowed to reverberate in the mind. It would be absurd to go to H.M. Stationery Office and buy the *Report of the Standing Committee respecting Umbrella Handles*, even though it costs only 8d.

Like some profoundly still Chinese vase, a title like this is a refuge. One steps into a quiet yet tremendously real world (nothing is more real than an umbrella; it resembles a bat, but bats twink out of sight in the gloaming, you can't hold a bat the way you can hold an umbrella—and of course bats don't keep the rain out).

Everyone will have his own idea. Mine is a sort of

private television serial—moving but static, real and dreamlike, the same situation endlessly elaborated. I have the clearest picture of the committee's permanent office. It is on the first floor in the vague district between Grays Inn Road and Southampton Row, where the large, smartly painted Georgian houses now turned into offices are interspersed by smaller ones still lived in. There is still a faint sense of neighbourhood; corner newsagents with green fascia-boards, area railings, even an occasional whiff of cabbage on Sundays; the new brutalist block, fences, hoardings, warehouses full of dusty pamphlets, medical accessories, small chromium things. Miles from any park or tree, utterly urban, anonymous. London.

The chairman is Benson Benson, 69, a lawyer, long-faced, prominent cheekbones, gold-rimmed glasses, dry sense of humour. Deep down he thinks there should really be only one kind of umbrella handle, the simple walking-stick-type hook, with a gold band, that is on his own. But strong-faced Thorold Parkson, 56, knows that times are changing. His great-grandfather founded Parkson's Umbrellas in Manchester (my encyclopaedia says umbrellas are manufactured 'mainly in London, Glasgow, Manchester, Paris and Lyons') but today Thorold manages the factory built on Western Avenue in 1937. He has recently been persuaded by his advertising agents to accept a complete restyling, even to the withdrawal of the trademark, famous in the twenties and thirties, of a little drawing of an umbrella with underneath it the words *Famous since the rain of Queen Victoria*. Parkson's wife, Yvonne, is French, daughter of a Lyons silk merchant whom he met on a business trip in 1936.

In the past there have been many heated arguments between him and Eddie Leibovitch, 41, balding, diamond tie-pin, double-breasted suit, who with £100 capital started the now well-known firm of Brollity Ltd. (factories at Edmonton and Hirwaun Trading Estate in Wales), which claims to make 'every other British brolly' and has massive contacts with the big chain stores.

The moderating influence between them has been Roger Preston, the *ex-officio* member from the Board of Trade, a career civil servant of 34, unmarried. For the past two years he has occasionally taken the commitee's secretary, Hester Folsom, 32, to a theatre and dinner, and when alone Hester often takes off her almond-shaped glasses, pats her hair, stares into the mirror and wonders if she really attracts him.

Today, however, Parkson and Leibovitch are united in their hatred of the newest member wished on to them, Kathy Fant, three months out of Camberwell Art School and already a power in the umbrella world. Not only has she insisted, at a stormy meeting, that umbrellas ending in chic little stainless steel hooks instead of ferrules could be hung up to dry; she has rudely denied Benson Benson's mild suggestion that the hooks would catch in the hats or trousers of passersby by retorting '*Your* umbrella handle is a hook, dad, only bigger.'

The usually diplomatic Roger has become besotted with this chit and has arranged to take her to a discothèque. The others are enraged. Until Fant's appearance (everyone including herself, refers to her thus) they have all taken their elevenses together at a comfortable old-fashioned place up the road, where white letters on the steamy plate-glass window, above the lace curtain, proclaim NOTED FO THE BEST CUP OF TEA IN THE   STRICT. But Fant insists on a coffee bar near the *Sunday Times* office. This morning, when kindly, rotund, middle-aged Fo bustles up to serve them he says, innocently, 'Good morning, Missee Folsom, gentlemen. Mister Pleston not here?' Hester burst into tears.

'It's intolerable,' says Benson Benson. 'The fellow's behaving like a cad.'

'Maybe Mister Pleston soon see Fant not worth botheling about, come back to Missee Folsom, say he velly solly.'

'You are kind, Fo. I'm sorry, everyone,' says Hester, wiping her eyes. 'Perhaps he was just being kind all this time, taking me to the D'Oyly Carte and everything.'

'You can take the day off if you like, Miss Folsom,' says Benson Benson kindly. 'We've got to go through the Regional Preference breakdown before we report to the Minister, and I don't think we shall have anything ready to dictate by today.'

'It just ain't true chubbies only go in the south' says Eddie Leibovitch. He taps a thick file. 'Look here, Mr Benson. I can show you. I got reports from my boys in Glasgow, Gateshead, Oban, places like that. Look—'

'Let's discuss it in the office, Leibovitch,' says Benson tactfully. Eddie gets up to leave with him, and says to Hester: 'Don't worry, kid. All that fancy talk and them schools he went to don't mean a thing if he goes off with the first bit of skirt that shows up. You want to get shot of him.'

'Uncouth lout!' says Thorold Parkson, who has stayed at the table with Hester. He feels he ought to go with them, even though it will only mean an acrimonious reopening of an old argument, for at Parkson's it is still thought that hooked handles are for men, chubbies for women, with no particular regional preferences, and he does not want the mass-produced Brollity range, with their vast chain-store sales, to blur the distinction still preserved in the quality range. But there is something he needs to discuss privately with Hester.

'Oh, Mr Leibovitch is a rough diamond, but he meant it kindly,' says Hester.

Parkson stares moodily into his green tea. 'Look, Miss Folsom—or do you mind if I call you Hester?' he says. 'I agree with him for once. He may well be right about Preston. I—I hope you will not think this is an inopportune moment for me to ask if you would, er, do me the honour of coming to "The Sound of Music" tonight?'

'But—your wife, Mr Parkson?'

'Yvonne and I have grown apart. She resents the time I've had to give to building up Parkson's. She's French, you know. She was young and gay when I married her (neither of her parents were natives of Lyons); used to the best of everything, skiing every year and so on. And somehow, over the years—'

Hester puts her hand gently over Parkson's. Her eyes are blurred with tears, or whatever it is in that bottle from Make-up. 'It's kind of you, Mr—Thorold.

But you know this wouldn't be right for either of us. You must go back to your wife. . . .'

Parkson does take his wife out that night, and afterwards over dinner at a little place in Soho, they are greeted by Henri, 30 years older now, with delight.

'Oh, Henri, ze place 'asn't changed at all.' Later, over the liqueur. 'Ah, T'orol', I 'ave been so un'appy when you 'ave been cold.'

'Things are going to be different from now on, Yvonne. Chap at the club, my age, started skiing last year, says it's not too old. . . .'

The next morning Hester Folsom does not turn up, her first absence since the committee was established. It is Kathy Fant who, when Hester's 'phone does not answer, drives round to the bed-sitter in her smart red Mini and finds Hester unconscious after an overdose of sleeping pills, and swiftly and efficiently arranges for medical help. She stays with her till she comes round, and tactfully withdraws when a remorseful Roger arrives for a bedside reconciliation.

She is surprised to find Benson Benson waiting outside in his Rover. 'Er, irregular, of course, but, er, thought I'd better see if she'd be all right. Been through quite a time, you know.'

Tough, brittle Fant breaks down and weeps into Benson's lapels. 'Darling Mr Benson, you've all been so kind, and I've been so awful.'

'Nonsense, child, we all have to grow up. And you may be right about those ferrules. Got to move with the times, eh? Here, take this handkerchief. . . .'

And so on. And on. And on. Till the ratings fall.

❡ Their Aunt Enough

◆◆◆◆◆◆◆◆◆◆◆◆◆◆◆◆◆◆◆◆◆◆◆◆◆◆◆◆◆◆◆◆◆◆◆◆◆

I WAS mistaken, of course, about the song announced
on the radio in the hotel bedroom as *I left my aunt in
San Francisco*. The picture must be reluctantly abandoned of this little apple-cheeked old aunt browsing
sadly through yellowing photographs of her brilliant
but wayward nephew, in the airless attic of a poor frame
house (you can see *how* reluctantly the picture is
abandoned) in a cheap part of the great city, with no
view of the Golden Gate, only of used car lots, waste
ground bordered by shops full of dusty reconditioned
dynamos, by sordid cheap wine bars and 24-hour false
teeth repair establishments. It was, of course, his *heart*,
not his aunt, that the singer left in San Francisco.

But I was not mistaken about the newspaper placard
last week. It was all over London:—

AUNT FOR ESCAPED GUNMAN

This is welcome, if belated, official recognition of the
vital importance of the aunt-figure in our Western
society, which other sociologists beside myself have
emphasized. As early as 1937 Fry and Toblerone, in
their pioneer study of the aunts of Liverpool, wrote:—

'For generations society has been stable enough to
provide a pool of aunts, by whom many of the oral
traditions of a culture are handed on. We reject the
distinction made by Heim-Süssheim between 'primary'
(unmarried) and 'secondary' (married) aunts. Quite
apart from the fact that if this were a valid distinction

it would be necessary to subdivide further into aunts with and without their own children, it misinterprets the mediating role of the aunt, which derives from her position inside the phratry or totem group but outside D.P.O. (Direct Parent Orbit) tension *as far as the nephew or niece is concerned*, and her own marital status is therefore irrelevant.'

Fry and Toblerone, incidently, quote a very significant girls' skipping rhyme from Liverpool, which has been unaccountably overlooked by the Opies and other collectors:—

> *Me mam told me this*
> *But me auntie told me that*
> *One feller wants a kiss*
> *And one's a dirty rat*

Schutt's well-known work in Cologne and, later, Milwaukee, arrived at the same conclusions as Fry and Toblerone in their latest and most massive survey, 'Aunts and Delinquency in a New Town', from which I quote the following table:—

Year	No. of Aunts	No. of offences by persons under 18
1956	743	1,273
1957	659	1,352
1958	657	1,360
1959	341	3,753

Some critics deny the conclusions drawn by Fry and Toblerone from these figures. As T. W. Carper wrote

in the *Sociological Review*, 'we are not shown *why* there
was such an exodus of aunts in 1959. Many (though not
all) aunts are elderly or retired women. Might we not
equally assume that, coming to the New Town in
1956, they found that although their picture of a
modern Utopia of pleasant dwellings grouped among
trees saved from the original farmland was visually
correct, socially it was not? May we not envisage them
sitting, afraid to go out, as they listened to gangs of
youths roaming through the night with an offence-rate
already approaching 2 per aunt per annum, greatly
in excess of the national norm? Might this not be why
nearly half of them left in a body when the delinquency-
explosion they had been dreading finally came in 1959?
We could thus say that delinquency had *caused* a lack
of aunts, not the other way round. Indeed Dr Fry and
Mr Toblerone seem to anticipate this objection, since
they naïvely write 'who knows how much the
delinquency-rate would have been reduced if the aunts
had stayed? Who, indeed? Professional sociologists will
be wary of such easy assumptions.'

Although this controversy has caused a deep split
in the sociological world, even Carper, of course, does
not deny the importance of aunts; and it is heartening
to see from that news placard that this country's lead
in applying these discoveries to our fractured society is
now bearing practical fruit. I visited the Home Office's
Aunt Training Centre shortly after its inauguration in
1961. As the principal, a pleasant, grey-haired woman
identified by her lapel badge as Auntie Betty ('we never
use surnames'), showed me round, I was impressed by

the extraordinary fluidity of the teaching. Although there were instructors in everything from abnormal psychology to knitting there were no formal classes. The instructors would mingle with the real and trainee aunts as they congregated in spontaneous social groups, in the flats of widely varying social standards into which the Victorian mansion had been converted.

It seemed revolutionary to me, but Auntie Betty was not satisfied. 'If only we could have some trainee gun-men!' she sighted. 'How can you train aunts for their natural function of helping and listening if they can practise only on other aunts?' Perhaps this will come. In the meantime we can all acclaim a step in the right direction.

> "Franco has imposed restriction after restriction on the passage of travellers' vehicles over the frontier at La Linea. The last straw is considered to be his order last Wednesday to downgrade the customs post at La Linea to third grade."
>
> —Sunday Times.

EXCEPT FOR the neon time-switch, everything seemed in order to Don Miguel. The automatic barrier, operated from a transmitting device in his car, swung up to admit him. The two immaculately turned-out sentries, from the crack 3rd Castilian Lancers, crashed to the salute simultaneously, perfectly.

He decided to walk to his office. *'Buenos dias, Señor Jefe,'* said the smart orderly who instantly appeared to drive his car round to the executive park. There was the promise of a wonderful day. A few gentle cumulo-nimbus clouds moved slowly eastward over the perfect blue bay, bringing a hint of Atlantic freshness, a suggestion of the vast adventure of the world, to the ancient and inward-dreaming Peninsula. A smooth path of rolled red gravel, flanked by a brilliantly whitewashed low wall, trim flower-beds, and lawns kept brilliantly green by the sprinklers already sparkling in the morning sun, led to the imposing main block. The neon sign, ADUANA: BIENVENIDO was still switched on. To the right was the laboratory block which he had put up in 1959; he noted with pleasure that the bougainvilia spilling over its white walls had really matured this year. To the left was the great new transit block, through which the road ran; air-conditioned examination hall and restaurant, waiting lounge and pleasure gardens. Workmen were adding the finishing touches to the elegant little white-pillared, gold-domed bandstand. At this hour discreetly exciting recorded music mingled with the plash of the fountains.

In the marble-pillared vestibule Don Miguel glanced, as he did every morning, at the plaque inscribed LA LINEA CUSTOMS POST, AWARDED FIRST PRIZE FOR EFFICIENCY AND BEAUTY (FIRST GRADE SECTION) BY MINISTRY OF TOURIST CULTURE. Concepcion, the ravishing receptionist (she was this year's Miss Algeciras) forestalled any complaint about the neon sign. 'We all noticed it, Señor Jefe. Enrique says it often happens in new installations. It is a matter of a new condenser. He is working on it now.'

Don Miguel nodded and went into his office. A lurking fear that had been with him for months now grew into panic, and his heart stood still when he saw the ominous sealed letter from the Madrid bag on his desk. It had come at last. He knew what the message was even as he broke the seals with trembling fingers, but all the same the curtness of the wording shocked him. *La Linea customs post is hereby downgraded to third grade as from Monday next. Staff instructions will follow shortly.*

There was a tap on the door and Senior Customs Scientific Officer Ramon Oreja-Nariz Y Garganta entered. A good boy, thought the Jefe, looking at the aristocratic, El Greco face cast in the lineaments of one of Spain's oldest families; nothing decadent there, the boy worked his way up, knows his stuff. Good prospects here, until this damned Gibraltar business started. Couldn't wish a better husband for Dolores. But now—

'Got a lorry outside,' said Ramon. 'Usual stuff. Hosiery latch needles, beakers, flasks, burettes, tubing and other lamp-blow ware, aircraft and parts thereof, manufactures of cotton wool (including alpaca, mohair, cashmere, llama, vicuña and camel's hair), hatter's fur (unblown), and a few wooden golf club heads roughly shaped by sawing but not further manufactured. Standard drawback rates, of course. But I thought I'd check with you about the surgeon's and post-mortem gloves, youth's wellington boots (dull) and babies' (toddlers') wellington boots (bright). Consignor claims minimum drawback for hydro-carbon oil content, but we've done a lab test, it's 7.53 in the wellingtons. Shall I send a signal?'

I'm getting old, thought Miguel. Wellington. He was on our side. The boy knows more than I do, anyway; couldn't follow all that about duty evasion on high polarization sugar by invert addition yesterday. Things were simpler when I started building this place up from the tin shack it was in '37. . . .

He became aware that Ramon was looking at him anxiously and pulled out of his reverie. 'Look here, Ramon, you must put in for Irun before anyone else does. We're finished here—you, I, all of us. Take a look at this.' He pushed the Madrid order across the desk.

Ramon paled. 'But sir, what about you? I couldn't ask Dolores to come to the other end of Spain. It would break her heart to be so far from you.'

'If you love her, and me, you will go,' said Don Miguel. 'Irun is First Grade, and likely to remain so. You must think of the future. I shall stay here. I retire in three years, anyway. I can't leave La Linea now. It is my life. But you are young. I'll stick it out. Perhaps the British will give it us. Perhaps Franco will die. Or that man Brown will do something. Things may change. . . .'

With a heavy heart Ramon agreed. The next six months were hectic, what with the move, settling in at Irun, and the birth of their first child. Don Miguel's letters were cheerful at first; he wrote of the challenge involved in keeping up standards with a greatly reduced allocation. But gradually the letters became gloomier, and there were increasingly bitter references to someone called El Sordido. Finally the letters ceased altogether. After four of their letters, and then two urgent telegrams, had failed to produce a reply, Ramon took a week's leave and set off alone, in their smart new Seat saloon, for La Linea.

When he finally drove up the familiar road from Algeciras to the post his worst fears were confirmed. A surly unshaven guard, with one epaulette missing from his crumpled, nineteenth-century-looking uniform and with his collar unbuttoned, examined Ramon's pass and grudgingly admitted him. Scrawny chickens squawked in and out among the goats tethered in the lank brown grass where the lawns had been. A slatternly, moustachioed widow in rusty black bombazine sat at the rough wooden table that had replaced Concepcion's elegant desk. Grubby barefoot children stared at him from the doors of huts built on the old pleasure grounds. In the hot, airless and indescribably filthy examination hall, tattered, yellow, fly-blown notices on the walls offered rewards for Carlist insurrectionists, prohibited the import of lucifer matches, sulphur, guano, whalebone bustles, obscene daguerreotypes and distempered mules. Long queues of cars stretched back to the Rock. Unshaven customs men wrenched off air filters and even carburettors from any car driven by a pretty woman, saying with a leer that these were well-known places for hiding opium. A male driver was led off to a padlocked room at the end of a corridor, marked INTERROGACION. There were flies everywhere.

Ramon found Miguel in his old office. He was still nominally in control, and this was an oasis of threadbare neatness, only evidence of former days. Miguel, hollow-cheeked, looked twenty years older. 'El Sordido does what he likes,' he whispered. 'God knows where Madrid dug him up. He's a gipsy, you know. Half the tribe came. They keep women in the old laboratory block. It's quiet enough there now, I expect they're all sleeping it off. But my God, you should hear the row at night, when they have their camp fires going. He's in with the smugglers too. I found this out and sent a minute to Madrid, and he got to hear of it. Perhaps they told him. I'm in fear of my life.'

'I've come to fetch you,' said Ramon simply. 'I've got a bit of pull in Madrid now. I called on the way, they've agreed to retire you now with full pension. There's room for you in our house, old man, and a seat in the garden, and you shall play with your grandson. Dolores and I have planned it all.'

They stopped the car on the road to Algeciras. Don Miguel looked back for the last time over the blue water at the great Rock and the distant buildings. He straightened his back. 'Some day, some day, it will be First Grade again,' he murmured. 'We shall return.' There was a moment's silence. Then the two men got into the car for the long journey north.

VERSE

☾ Where the Bee Stuck

✦✦✦✦✦✦✦✦✦✦✦✦✦✦✦✦✦✦✦✦✦✦✦✦✦✦✦✦✦✦✦

Bee
How glad I am to be me!
That is to say, not to be a bee;
You silly ass
That window is made of glass,
Can't you see that, can't you see,
You silly bee?
All day long you have made a buzzing, a
                        bumbling, a fuss, a ruction,
A small worry, a worry to me:
Are you just going to try to push through it,
                     buzzing there till you die?
Unlike you, bee, I have powers of deduction,
I'd have said, if I were a bee
(That is to say, a man in the shape of a bee
Which God forbid), not just a bee like you,
I'd have said 'I don't know what the hell this is,
     that you can see through but you can't fly through
But I can see there is no use at all
In running my head against a brick, that is to say
                a glass (or whatever the hell it is) wall.'
I should go into a corner and think, or possibly pray.
I should say
'Here is a game which logic, not doggedness, that
              is to say bee-edness, will win,
All I must do is remember how I got in . . .'

153

Instead of which, again and again
You angrily, busily scrabble up the pane
And busily buzz and fall, again and again.

Listen, you bee,
Clearing the cold window-sill in January
I have found, all furry and dusty
Bees, as dead as dead,
Bees that were once as lusty
And as idiotic as you.

Why, though you slightly give me the creeps,
Do I want to help you out?
O, I've read all about
Bees, although your sex is something that keeps
Confusing me, you all look so hairy and male,
           like very small Nubian robots; yet male:

Virgil, when of bees he sings
Always describes your Queens as kings.
I'm sorry you don't know, you bee, you female
           (Good Lord!), you worker bee
That if you ate that royal jelly, with Vitamin E
You'd be a Queen.
I'm sorry for the one male in a swarm who can fly as
    high as the Queen, whom he is then allowed to wed
After which he falls down dead;
It's obscene.
I'd be a hymen-opter-out—*Hymenoptera*, you see?—
—(No, sorry, one shouldn't tell jokes to a bee).

And though I make no bones
About my attitude to your attitude to drones

I am also sorry you bees
Are subject to something called *Isle of Wight disease*
Which, if I have got it right, is
A kind of bee bronchitis
(It must be funny to hear bees
Cough and sneeze).

Good Lord, are you at it still,
Clambering up from the window sill?
And heavens, now there's *another* bee crawling
                                        outside
Like your reflection. Is he, I mean she, trying
                                        to get inside,
Sent from that fearful humming hive
To see where you are, and if you're still alive?
(I'm sorry you don't know that your directional dance
Recently discovered by K. von Frisch, is to us
a marvel, a proof, an omen, a revelation, a thing
                                        to absorb and entrance;
I just wish
You knew about K. von Frisch).

If I were a bee-sized man, unable to think,
And you were a man-sized bee, with my
                                        deductive brain.
And I were scrabbling at the windowpane
(What a ghastly thought, me less than
                                        an inch, all pink,
And you with your frightful sacs and
                                        mandibles and things
Some six feet wide, with outstretched wings!)
Would you, bee, you buzzing bumbler,

Get, as I get for you, a tumbler
(Your outside friend has gone, I see),
    Clap it over (shut up, bee,
I'm *helping* you), and slide this card
Across the top (don't buzz so hard,
I'm *saving* you), and go downstairs,
And free me into summer airs?
Would you, bee? Ah, bee, you might
Care less to set the world aright
Than man does. And I tell you, bee,
He only cares occasionally.

ℭ Poetagoonia

International Expedition of Poets and Others
departs from Cape Horn for Patagonia August 1.
Contact HAM 5721.
> The Times, personal column, July 7.

But why Patagonia, lonely and peopled with sheep,
So bony and stony a zone? Why pneumonia
Zanier, loonier poets? The Andes are steep
In chillier, rainier west Patagonia
(Owned, did you know it, by Chile; an
                                omen in name!),
And, mainly through drainage, the north
                                (Argentinian),
Windier, wilder than Wales whence they came,
Of Welshmen and sheep is the weal and dominion.
Should your *koinonia* (fellowship), poets, not be
Mediterranean? In Patagonia
(This is a platitude) latitudes do not agree
With blazing azalea, pots of begonia:
No bougainvilias this part of Chile adorn;
Remote is the lotos! No isle Tennysonian
For sailors in whalers in gales off Cape Horn
(Erroneous poets!), or shores Patagonian!
Would not symposia held in a cosier land,
Not sterner and wilder than heaths Caledonian
Net you a peppier, hippier, happier band
Of bards Dionysian or Apollonian?
Surely these Others (not Poets?) who
                                go on this trip,

Unless schizophrenia, madness or mania
Addles their crania, won't sail the main in a ship,
Be it as famed as the old *Mauretania*,
Simply to listen to lyrics, dactylic or terse,
To epics and varia, mad miscellanea
In areas bare with an air unconducive to verse?
Why not Rumania, even Tanzania?
Catalonia, say? Or by purple Tyrrhenian seas?
That's where your hearers would find it
                      much cheerier;
Why ever should *they* go to Tierra del Fuego,
Where in the world is it wilder or drearier?
Why Patagonia? Was it nostalgia for myth?
(The early inhabitants, known as Tehuelches
Were giants, now vanished. The Spanish
                word [furnished herewith—
Patagones] means *very big feet*; what the Welsh is
My seedier encyclopaedia doesn't reveal,
Or whether they've other myths there
                    in a plethora).
But surely, you know, if the poets do go, it's to feel
Lonelier, rather than gathered-togetherer;
All poets, you'll own, are alone;
                and they certainly will
Groan at the tone of your plan Babylonian,
Masses of passages booked to Parnassus—a hill
Patently, blatantly not *Patagonian*.

ℂ Stiwdio B

(A non-U verse)

━━━━━━━━━━━━━━━━━━━━━━━━━━━━━━━━━━━━

It's a ciwrious thing about Stiwdio B;
In the niwspaper columns it seems to obtriwde
                                    quite undiwly
Where they tell yiw what's diw to be shown on TV
It catches the eye. Do they spell it so,
                            really and triwly?

In biwtiful Wales
What viwing prevails—
Siwrely siwperior stuff to the stock BBC

Viewed from Carlisle to N.W.3?
Siwrely in Stiwdio B there were cries of 'Iwreka!
Biwty and triwth, from all platitiwdes free
Niw viws will we give to yiwr screen, and
                            niw tiwnes to yiwr speaker!
To yiwr set yiw'll be gliwd—
Nothing shoddy or criwd,
No liwdness—although we're not priwdish
                                    in Stiwdio B!

None are more fiwrious and fiwming than we
To see the misiwse of TV, and the lack
                                    of invention,
The piwny, jejiwne, psiwdo-*dernier-cri*,
Deliwded attempts to amiwse. It's our aim
                                    and intention
The viwers to thrill
From Niwport to Rhyl,

So hiwgely profiwse are our good niw ideas.

                                   Ah, yiw'll see.

No more need yiw bow to the stiwpid decree

Of the ratings; for, diwped by their liwdicrous

                                 power, the viwer

Has too long been assiwmed to be brained like a flea,

Too long has he stared in a stiwpor at plays

                                 from the siwer,

At interviws riwd,

At old films reniwed,

At iwseless old miwsic-hall, serials boring or twee.

But do not dediwce that from Stiwdio B

Wilissiw a tissiw of stuff for the fiw, not the many.

TV's iwniversal, we're siwre yiw'll agree;

Of diwtiful fiwgal diwets there'll be little, if any—

Though miming by miwts

In Carnaby siwts

Is also precliwded, as *not* being our cup of tea.

Niw dociwmentary fiwsion yiw'll see

Of Miwsic (iwphoniums! tiwbas!), the niws,

                              and the mountains,

And miners exiwberant out on a spree;

The miwses of Wales will reniw you from

                              innocent fountains . . .'

Ah, Stiwdio B.

I assiwme this with glee

Because I don't viw yiw. I live much too far to the E.

❡ Jet, but not Black

✦✦✦✦✦✦✦✦✦✦✦✦✦✦✦✦✦✦✦✦✦✦✦✦✦✦✦✦✦✦✦

Fountain: wonderful watery whispering
                              madrigal in air,
Rising roulade and fa-la-la falling;
Fountain: shape of a sound, of a limpidly lilting
                              lull to care,
Still as a stone, but burbling and brawling;
Fountain: neutral and nerveless and null, in a
                              weeping far from woes,
Lisping in lovely alliteration
Meaning nothing but singing in silence, or dance
                              where stillness flows,
Legato but lively, endless libation
Poured to graceful and shadowy names—
                              Arethusa, Muses, Pan,
Charming by water lest dry hearts harden;
Fountain: solace and sister-glissando to
                              music mute in man,
How did it come to dance in my garden?

              I bought it in the Euston Road,
              A little leaden fellow,
              Copied, as the leaflet showed,
              From one by Donatello:
              A trip to Gamages' to buy
              A fractional-h.p. pump,
              Some pipes of polythene, and I
              Was ready for the jump
              Into the fountain-owning class;

Into *my* pond would patter
Home-made sunlit rain. Alas,
I overlooked one matter—

Twice a year I must dabble and grovel in nasty
                                    noisome ooze,
Cleaning it out and changing the water;
Twice a year I must wangle with wirework
                          a cover, although this ruse
Stops not a son, stops never a daughter
Under seven, from dropping and dumping their
                              baubles, bricks and toys.
Aeroplanes, boats with manikins plastic,
Tea-spoons, bicycle pumps and a twenty-year-old
                                    Big Book for Boys
Sunk in a glugsome horror fantastic.
See! The siphoned-off (sucked through a
                      hose to commence it) sordid stew
Slowly reveals a jetsam disgusting—
Slime-encrusted, the egg-whisk (I ought to have
                          guessed I'd find that too),
Good kitchen knives once sharp, but now rusting!
See! In not-very-long-ago-crystalline water
                                now there squirm
Sinister animalculae madly
Darting, desperate now as the level drops
                      (*Yugs!* A quite dead worm!)
Down to the bit I'd like leave alone gladly!
Whence this uggery-gluggery mud? Is it only
                              last year's leaves?
How can a pond cleaned out in the autumn

Fill so soon (through a chicken-wire cover)
                with sludge whence one retrieves
Toys gone astray since godparents bought 'em?

Fountain: wonderful watery whispering
                         madrigal in air,
Gracing my garden, presence which blesses,
Children also are fair, but a man cannot
                    savour what is fair
Till he has learnt what horrible mess is.

WAR AND PEACE

⁅ The Unforgiving Second

✦✦✦✦✦✦✦✦✦✦✦✦✦✦✦✦✦✦✦✦✦✦✦✦✦✦✦✦✦✦✦✦✦✦✦

> The United States Army has developed an
> atomic clock capable of marking one thousand
> millionth of a second. The clock, about a cubic
> foot in size, will gain or lose only one second in
> three hundred years. Weighing forty-four pounds, it
> is rugged enough for use in the field and can be
> handled by one man.

THAT'S WHAT I read not all that long ago in *The
Times*. I've been worrying about it ever since. I see
a command post deep in some continent disused except
for some peasants in grey sacks. Captain Crackafeller,
U.S. Army, decorated for bravery in World War II
as a sergeant, still lean and active, is pacing restlessly.
An intelligence officer, Captain Eikopf, is peering
through binoculars across no-man's-land.

Crack.: Hell of a World War Three this turned out to
be. Four months in this God-forsaken country and
we still never get orders to begin. Whyn't we just lay
into those bastards over there? We're the United
Nations, aren't we?

Eikopf: That's the trouble. They say *they're* the
United Nations. It got very confusing after the Chinese
were let in.

Crack.: Listen, this outfit was sent here by the
Pentagon, not the goddam Chinese. The Pentagon know
which is the United Nations, don't they?

164

Eikopf (*softly: he has seen something terrible through the glasses*): Maybe they're waiting till we've all got the new weapon.

Crack.: Well, I've got news for you. It's come. It came yesterday. You know what it is? It's a goddam clock.

Eikopf (*to himself*): So! They've done it. They've broken the dream.

Crack.: What's that?

Eikopf (*hastily*): Nothing, nothing. A clock, you said?

Crack.: Yeah, a clock. Biggest damn clock you ever saw. What are we supposed to do with it?

Eikopf: Perhaps we could set it wrong and parachute it on the enemy so that they didn't know what the time was.

Crack.: Listen, don't tell me. Those guys can tell the time with water, and candles, and like that. They *invented* clocks, I read it in the *Reader's Digest*.

Eikopf: Did anyone come with it?

Crack: Yeah, there was some sergeant brought it. They even made this new rank for it. Clock Sergeant. (*Muttering*) We never had any of *them* in the old Fighting Fifth.

Enter the Clock Sergeant. He conveys a curious air of premature age; a strong muscular figure but the face of a baby who knows too much.

Clock Serg. (*in a sing-song voice*): Clock Sergeant No. 47 reporting sir. Here are my credentials, from which you will observe that I am not authorized to divulge my name. Please address me simply as 'Clock Sergeant.'

Crack.: You don't look like a soldier at all to me.

Clock Serg.: Sir, if you would care to equip three of

your toughest veterans with a burden of one cubic foot weighing forty-four pounds, and see which of us gets back first from that—

Crack. (*warned by something in the Clock Sergeant's eyes*): O.K., O.K., so you're trained. Well, tell me about this clock. How do you wind it up? I guess most of that forty-four pounds, is lead, eh? I read a piece in the *Reader's Digest*, you got to have all this lead to absorb the neutrons. Or was it the protons? I guess there's just a little bitty atomic wristwatch inside all that lead, eh? Well, I'll be darned, an atomic clock. What'll you guys think of next?

Clock Serg.: It can measure one thousand millionth of a second.

Crack.: Say, I've got an idea. We could get the artillery guys, we could synchronize their watches so darn tightly they could fire a hundred guns off in the same millionth of a second, KROW! And those bastards over there would think it was only one gun.

Clock Serg. (*absently*): It's feasible, sir.

Three hundred artillery officers are summoned.

Crack.: Now, you guys, stand in a line, from north to south. The Clock Sergeant here says this thing is so accurate, if one guy stands five yards west of another he's in a different time. Right. Are you ready? On the pip it will be 1428.6730459 hours.

The Clock Sergeant fiddles with a dial.

Clock Serg.: There you are, gentlemen.

Crack.: I didn't hear anything.

Cock Serg.: Of course not, sir. The human ear can't register a pip lasting one thousand millionth of a second.

Eikopf (*still looking through binoculars*): I *thought* so. Those are Americans on the other side. And I can see a man with a rugged-looking thing about a cubic foot—

Clock Serg.: Yes; he's French, as it happens. But most of us are American. We're all tuned in.

Eikopf: And you've found Zeno was right.

Clock Serg.: I see you understand. (*To Crackafeller*) You see, sir, Zeno was among the first thinkers to ask if time, change, the multiplicity of space, were not all illusion; the famous Paradox of Zeno. According to Zeno a moving arrow—

Eikopf: Or a moving bullet.

Clock Serg.: —or a moving bullet, doesn't really move at all, because at any point in time, if that point is infinitely small, it must be at that point, and therefore not moving. Well, Rutherford split the atom spatially, and we've done it with time; we have split the second. In a few moments a master signal will go out to all the atomic clocks in all the world's armies at all the tension points. And humanity's rush to destruction will be halted. Except for certain moral leaders, the Optimi, already chosen, who will be in a protective lead chamber—

Crack.: Ha, I was right about that lead, wasn't I?

Clock Serg.: —all humanity will be—not destroyed, but frozen in an immoveable non-instant of time. Alone the Optimi—

Eikopf: Are you one of them?

Clock Serg.: Oh no, I'm not nearly good enough. I'm just proud to serve them. Alone the Optimi, able to use the illusion of time as it should be used—for harmony, the growth of life—will work on the as yet un-imaginable articulation of words, categories, laws, statements, possibly unanswerable music, so beautiful and real that humanity, when it is awakened and released into time again, perhaps by the children or even the grandchildren of the Optimi, will instantly see. They will fill time harmoniously, they will—

Crack.: Hey, wait! I want to be one of the Optimi. Do you think I *like* war? You think I haven't got kids, didn't leave 'em to come here because I thought we were right, you think I never got to thinking, when I see a sunset, I—

There is a curious sound, a kind of instantaneous sharp hum. All are frozen in mid-gesture, including the Clock Sergeant, on whose face there is a terrible, ravishing smile.

ℭ Singing is so Good a Thing

THURSDAY EVENING. Everybody in London except us seems to be going home, whatever fragmentary unity the City possesses is dissolving in this centrifugal, outward rush. This is our basic rehearsal evening. One here, one there, we move, converging against the homeward tide—a solitary figure on the up escalator at Warren Street, someone on a motor-scooter rounding Regent's Park, someone trying to park in Fitzroy Square, where mysterious drawing-boards are glimpsed in the basements of Georgian houses long since turned into offices.

The random many-ness and confusion of traffic is shut out as we pass through the plate-glass doors of (as it happens) the Indian Students' Union. Down the stairs to the foyer of its semi-basement hall. Now there is a many-ness of people; greetings, laughter, signing of attendance forms, under a large painting of (as it happens) Mahatma Gandhi. Someone has sandwiches and a flask of coffee (we shall be at it for nearly three hours).

Inside the hall the corporate sense of whatever it is that has brought us here grows minute by minute as the noise subsides. The last briefcase is closed, the last score is opened, a hand is raised, and out of the total silence there comes that mysterious fusion of many human breaths, so physical yet so mystical, the sound of a great chorus.

Although it has been fashionable for some critics to

imply that English choral singing was a sea of sloppy amateurism until Wilhelm Pitz set new standards with the Philharmonia, there are plenty of people in Huddersfield, Leeds, Glasgow, Magdalen College, Oxford, Westminster Cathedral and many other places who would indignantly and rightly deny this. We have always taken a pride in our choirs.

Nevertheless, what Herr Pitz has done is to give a professional precision and bite to an entirely amateur body. Any concert in which the New Philharmonia Chorus appears is usually sold out. This collection of clerks, teachers, housewives, engineers, and even journalists, for many of whom the Chorus is the central thing in their lives, often more thought about than their actual jobs, swallowing up travelling time, disembowelling family weekends, has made records which have several times been nominated for top awards by (for instance) America's National Institute of Recorded Arts and Sciences.

The role of chorus-master is a curious one in the world of music. Having brought a work as near to perfection as he can, after an early conference with the orchestral conductor at which the great man's wishes about interpretation are ascertained, he has to hand over the instrument he has forged on the night when the dinner-jackets and the little black dresses are worn and the hall begins to fill with a great audience. But, of course, he is utterly identified with the chorus, and it with him.

Singing for nearly 20 years now, an obscure second tenor third from the left in some middle row—first under Charles Kennedy Scott in the now defunct Oriana Madrigal Society and now under Pitz—I have noticed that the thing about this kind of genius is not that he is far out, with a special and unique theory, but rather that he sees the obvious more clearly than anyone else.

Although it is true that both men were fantastically different types—Scott a contemplative, Pitz an extrovert; Scott refining vowels, bending music to verbal rhythms, Pitz forever seeking absolute precision—one's reaction to almost any rehearsal point or modification made by either of them has always been *Yes, of course, that's natural*.

Pitz is a tremendous borrower of voices. Any score used in the New Philharmonia is covered with arrows leading to other parts. It seems obvious afterwards, and the Chorus sometimes sounds twice as big as it is.

Sometimes if a part is sung without feeling he will mimic it, bellowing or mooing. Then he will sing it himself, ever so slightly sharp, a seraphic expression on his rather cherubic face. The point is taken. *Ah, so is better. Now it is MOZART*. Off comes the coat, then the bow tie, then the collar. A driving sense of climax. *You must see, zis amen, it is like a flame, it leaps up, then the other part comes in ah, ah-ah-ah-AH-men. Put it in your part, so . . . When you say Sanctus, you call on God, not on Mr Smith. You call out louder each time. Sanctus, Sanctus, SANCTUS. Ozzerwise He will not come.*

It is always a wonderful moment when a work rehearsed for weeks like this to the piano (we have a particularly brilliant and sympathetic accompanist in Martin Penny) suddenly takes on magical depth and reality at the orchestra rehearsals; like colour after black and white. All those pages we have skipped blossom out into sinuous cello lines moulded by Giulini, a majestically controlled scherzo under Klemperer. The voices of world-famous soloists—Ludwig, Gedda, Höffgen, Ghiaurov, Gwynneth Jones—echo round some improbable place like Battersea Town Hall. We come out afterwards into the incurious chaotic street, I think *Ha, you Battersea, you little know what a sound we have been making in your midst.*

Very often the very last rehearsal is on Sunday morning at the Festival Hall. After all the preparation there's a sense here of a kind of spiritual elbow-room. Everyone is in casual clothes, getting through empty London and parking has been easy, as in a dream; there's an audience of about six rows, relatives and friends with rehearsal tickets (two seats per member). One or two heart-stopping climaxes—the *Tuba mirum* fanfare in the Verdi *Requiem*, an entry, a great fugal climax—give thrilling promise of the night's effort, but for the most part it is relaxed, the smoothing-out of final details.

This is a final fusion of amateur and professional. No one in the Chorus could make a living as a performer, but here we are, united with one of the world's finest orchestras, in one of those supreme statements of and about man for which (was the *War Requiem* an anachronism?) one sometimes thinks sadly that the historical moment of creation has passed. In those great masses which seem to loom so large in our repertoire the tender and desperate Christian view of man is expressed with the new humanistic and technical confidence of the Enlightenment. Today's composers in their isolated scratchy mathematical little worlds don't seem to have the social confidence to assemble these vast expectant forces, the great rows of singers and the shining instruments under the towering organ.

In any case the sequence of thought in those timeless old words seems to mean just as much to an audience of modern agnostics ('It's much more terrifying if you don't believe in it,' said Colin Davis of the Mozart *Dies Irae* during a chorus rehearsal). *Tu solus sanctus*, 'Thou alone art holy,' can inspire the composer to some immense statement of grandeur and reality for which you do not have to be baptized; the ominous war-trumpets, the drum-beats and the desperate soprano cry that suddenly punctuate the calm strains of *dona nobis pacem*, 'grant us peace', at the end of the sublime Beethoven Mass mean a lot more to Bomb-conscious modern audiences than they did to the Victorians. Even on the level of mere drama, it is difficult to imagine anything more thrilling than the sorrowful vowel sounds, whispered by a hushed chorus, of *sepultus est*, 'He was buried', followed by the extraordinary sunburst that can be made with *et resurrexit*, 'and He rose again'.

In our two main conductors, Giulini and Klemperer, we have the two opposite approaches to music—the physical and the mental, the Apollonian and the Dionysiac, the Italian and German—wonderfully illustrated.

Klemperer, whom I suspect of buying special conductor's glasses in a shop in Stuttgart or somewhere that look straight at you—this man of 81, survivor of a tumour and of having set himself on fire, sitting at the place to which he has to be assisted, waving a shaky hand at rehearsal, calling on tenors or altos to give more ('I can't hear you, da ah ah parm parm', in a quavering and unrecognizable melodic fragment), has an imperious control that makes the great inevitable climaxes doubly exciting.

Stories, many doubtless apocryphal, cluster round his crusty and vaguely sardonic figure as they used to cluster round Beecham. He asked a young English composer, who had just written a symphony, what he thought of Dvorak's *New World*. Not much, the rash youth intimated. 'I know it is only old symphony from the New Vurld,' said Klemperer, a faint smile visible through those terrible glasses, 'but maybe it is better than new symphony from the Old Vurld.'

Giulini, before he starts the Verdi *Requiem* at all, screws the silence up to an almost unbearable intensity before releasing the cellos on the soft phrase that starts this clamorous, passionate and moving work; he lives in a kind of white-hot present, and one is constantly reminded by the way he expresses the music with his whole body that this is someone from a nation that has never heard of puritanism.

Real choral discipline, such as you get in the New Philharmonia, is a northern thing. It seems to fascinate the Italians. We did the Verdi *Requiem*, and the *Four Sacred Pieces*, for the 150th anniversary celebrations at Parma in 1963. The Teatro Reggio had been repainted white and gold for the occasion, and we were all a bit nervous of the notoriously partisan audience. In the event they wrote lyrically about *i complessi londinesi*, the London complex of forces, and said of their perfectly adequate Italian soloists that in fact it was difficult to find soloists good enough to stand in front of this lot. There were great banks of carnations in front of the boxes, which they rained down at the end, shouting until we did the *Sanctus* again.

I am writing about a work of love, and perhaps it is Giulini who loves the Chorus most. At the only purely Chorus rehearsal we had with him before the two performances in St Paul's for the City of London Festival, he joined in the laughter at the preliminary announcements ('There will be 2,700 in the audience, 80 in the orchestra and 218 in the Chorus. In the crypt there is one ladies' and one gentlemen's lavatory. You have been warned'). Then we began.

After the first number Giulini said, 'Ladies and gentlemen, you know what it is like, a memory? You know something, you cannot think what it is. When I am away, in Italy, I think often, what is the sound which the Philharmonia makes. What is it? Now I am here, you make it again. Now I remember. It is like a rose, you go in a garden, there is a beautiful rose, and then it is gone. But you come the next day, and there is another one, just as beautiful.'

As William Byrd wrote in the sixteenth century:—

> Since singing is so good a thing
> I wish all men would learn to sing.